Nothing Is Impossible

Nothing Is Impossible

By

Bernard Palmer

MOODY PRESS
CHICAGO

ISBN 0-8024-5963-3

Contents

Author's Note

Working on this book was a strange and rewarding experience. I have known Eugene and Ferne Clark for more than twenty-five years through my long association with Back to the Bible Broadcast. Yet I did not come to appreciate them fully until I began to do the interviews for this book.

Frankly, I was somewhat disturbed by the assignment in spite of being eager to have a part in telling the Clarks' story to others who face problems and tribulation. I thought the long hours of interviews would be depressing, and I wondered whether I would have difficulty keeping the gloom from my writing. I need not have been concerned.

The reader may wonder at the lack of discouragement in Eugene and Ferne Clark, and particularly in Eugene. I wondered myself. The deeper I went in the interviews, however, the more apparent it became that that is the way they are. God in His mercy has given them a peace and victory over circumstances that I have never seen in anyone else. I have portrayed the Clarks' lives as they came through in their own accounts and in the interviews I did with longtime friends and associates.

As I look at my own reaction to the trials that have come my way—trials that seem as nothing compared to those that these friends have faced—I am amazed at the serenity in the Clark home and the joy and happiness the entire family experiences. Their pastor, Curt Lehman, expressed it well: "I have found myself going to see Eugene, thinking to encourage him, but invariably I've been the one who has been encouraged and comforted. I couldn't begin to tell you how many times he has helped me."

BERNARD PALMER

1

"Why Not Us?"

The bitter wind blew along the wide thoroughfare
in Rochester, Minnesota, that winter of 1962, carrying a trace of snow with it. In February the plug
seemingly had been pulled on the bottom of the thermometer, and the mercury had plunged to a
numbing forty degrees below zero. Cars crept over
the icy pavement, clouds of smoke rising from their
exhaust pipes. People rushed along the walk,
bundled against the cold and eager to be inside
again.

Everyone was eager to get inside, that is, except
Ferne Clark. She was oblivious to the weather and
those around her, even though she was shivering in
her thin, threadbare coat. Waiting for a green light
on the corner, she tightened her grip on the package
under her arm and moved to her left to allow a
jaywalker to hurry past. She blinked and a tear
rolled down, quickly freezing on her frost-reddened
cheek.

The hospital was just across the intersection, and
her young husband, Eugene, was in one of the
rooms on the fourth floor, waiting impatiently for
bandages to be removed from his eyes. He was not
supposed to talk, so delicate had been the surgery

and so important it was that he not move any of the muscles of his slender, pain-scarred face. He was not even to have the radio on. But, all the precautions notwithstanding, the doctor had warned Ferne that the operation might not be successful, that Eugene might be blind.

The surgeons at the Mayo Clinic had twice refused to perform the operation because of the risk, and they had reluctantly decided to go through with it this time only because there seemed to be no other alternative to certain blindness. They had been brutally candid about the uncertainty of success as they explained the operation to Ferne.

Eugene had never tried to deceive Ferne about the uncertainty of his health. At the time he told her that he loved her and asked her to marry him, he told her as much as he knew about his physical condition. He even insisted that she talk to his doctor so that she would understand the situation and be sure of her decision. It was not lack of effort on the part of those who knew about his condition that kept her ignorant; it was her own determination that God would never allow such a tragedy to happen.

She had built a wall of fantasy around her husband and their little family that, to her, was impenetrable. She could talk about the fact that the threat was always with them, that they did not know what the next month or week, or even the next hour, held for them. The threat was always there, she could say, but her heart told her that those were just words. They were too happy, and God was too good to allow such a tragedy to strike them. She had prayed and firmly expected that Eugene and their children would be kept from harm. After all, how could her gangling, exuberant husband continue his work as director of music at the Back to the Bible Broadcast in Lincoln, Nebraska, without his sight? He was selecting music, arranging, and composing in addition to his responsibilities at the organ for the daily radio program.

Before she had known him, he had committed his life and his considerable musical ability to the service of Christ. His chief concern had been to serve God. As she had sat in the waiting room a few days before, keeping a lonely vigil while the doctors were working over Eugene, she had been too distraught to pray. But she had decided anew that God could never allow one who cared so much for Him to be struck blind.

We wouldn't do that to a loved one, she reasoned in desperation. *How can we expect less from our heavenly Father, who loved us so much that He sent His own Son to die on the cross for us?*

Now that the operation was over, however, and the long, tense period of waiting began, doubts crowded in to rob her of sleep and torment her endlessly. The surgeon had tried to be kind and gentle, but how could such a blow be softened? "I don't want either of you to build up your hopes, Mrs. Clark," he had said. "Eugene is walking along the edge of a precipice, even if he does keep his sight now. He could lose it at any moment from a new attack. That's one of the more ugly characteristics of iritis. No one knows why or when it will strike again, or how severe any given attack will be."

The light changed, and Ferne crossed the street and hurried into the lobby of the big hospital. It was almost time for dinner to be served, and she wanted to be there to feed her husband. Since the operation, she had jealously taken that responsibility from the nurse's aides, feeding him breakfast, lunch, and dinner. In fact, except for brief shopping trips such as the one she had just been on, she had been spending most of her waking hours in his room, from the time she came in to help him with his breakfast un-

11

til the nurses chased her out at eleven o'clock each night.

"Oh, it's cold out, Eugene," she said, shivering as she slipped out of her coat. "I thought I would freeze by the time I got here. I see they haven't brought you your dinner. I was afraid I wouldn't get here in time and you'd have to go hungry. That would have been a revolting development, now, wouldn't it?" She spoke brightly, as though he were responding to every comment.

And all the while the chief surgeon's words ran repeatedly through her bewildered mind. "The operation could leave Eugene blind." *It could leave him blind. Blind. Blind!* The doctor was too professional and kindly to remove the last trace of hope, but she knew, somehow, that he fully expected Eugene to lose his sight—if not now, then in another attack next week or next month or next year. But she could not allow her husband to sense her discouragement. She had to keep up the charade, the appearance of confidence.

"I got you some new pajamas today," she told him. "Wait until you see them! Wow! They're the brightest, reddest pajamas I could find." She had decided that if the operation was successful, she wanted him to see those pajamas just as soon as they removed the bandages. Later the idea seemed silly to her, but at the time it was all important. "I'll give them to the nurse so they can put them on you in the morning."

Eugene listened to her gay chattering and found himself encouraged by it. "I wish I could take off these bandages right now and see them," he said impulsively.

She laughed. "No way. You've got to wait to see them."

He reached out, his bony fingers seeking Ferne's firm hand. "Leave it to you to do something crazy

12

like buying me a pair of bright red pajamas," he said, chuckling. "We really don't have the money for such things."

"Shush. You're not supposed to talk, you know," she said. The laughter fled her voice. "You don't care, do you?"

"No. No, I don't care," he said. The last week or two had been rough for her. If she got any enjoyment out of buying him a pair of pajamas, that was all right with him.

He lay back on the pillow, only half listening to her lighthearted chatter. In his mind he could see the half-completed arrangement he had been working on the day before they left Lincoln for Rochester. He should have finished it before he left the office, he reasoned. Theodore Epp, his boss and the founder and general director of the Broadcast, had wanted to use that number with one of the messages he was preparing. Now someone would have to find another hymn or else finish his work, and he did not believe they would do the latter. Each arranger has a different style, a distinctive flair to his arrangements. The number would not sound right if another arranger took up where he left off and finished the work.

But that was not his greatest concern. Back to the Bible Broadcast had radio programs to produce and a responsibility to its donors to use wisely the money they gave. Lately it seemed that he had missed more days because of illness than he had worked. He wondered how much longer his employers would be able to carry him or what would happen if they finally decided they could no longer keep him on the staff. He had to think about his family. He and Ferne had two lively boys and a darling baby daughter to care for. If the Broadcast let him go, how would he be able to provide for his family? He had been praying much about the situation while he

13

lay in his doctor-imposed silence. He had to think about the possibility that he would lose his sight and most surely his position with the Broadcast. Little things like the pajamas Ferne had so impulsively bought for him helped to brighten his day and take his mind from the staggering problems the future might bring.

Although Eugene was wearing the pajamas when the time came for the bandages to be removed, they were not what he saw first. He was up and walking around by the time he noticed the pajamas. Eugene sat on a chair near the bed while the doctor took off the gauze covering. There was a tense moment as the final wrapping slipped away and Eugene's eyes were exposed to the light for the first time since the operation. Ferne's round face was white and drawn, and her lips trembled. Eugene looked around, blinking against the unfamiliar light. Then he stood mechanically, like one who had just awakened from a sound sleep.

"That picture!" he exclaimed, his voice strained by emotion. "It's not very clear yet, but it's of Christ!"

Ferne's eyes were wet with tears and her voice was robbed of sound, but a prayer went up: *Thank You, Lord. Thank You, Lord!* She had never felt so grateful.

For a time Eugene was completely unaware of the presence of anyone else in the room. Slowly he moved across the carpet and stood before the framed likeness of Jesus Christ. He drank in the magnificent beauty of the painting as though he had never expected to see anything like it again.

"There's the chestnut hair," he said quietly, "and the soft eyes. It's Sallman's *Head of Christ,* isn't it?"

By this time tears were streaming down Ferne's cheeks. She did not look at the surgeon, but for some reason she was aware that his eyes were also moist.

14

Eugene's sight did not completely return that day. There was a certain fuzziness about the objects he saw, and the shadows were opaque and blurred. Actually it was several weeks before he could see normally, but the doctor assured him that for the immediate future the prognosis was bright.

Finally, the time came for Eugene to be released so that he and Ferne could return to Lincoln. His dad, Hugh, came up by bus to drive back with them. The morning they left Rochester it started to snow, and before they were ten miles from the medical center they were in a blinding blizzard. They debated long about whether to go on, and finally they decided to drive as far as Sioux City, Iowa, where they would stop for the night. Every mile they drove, they passed cars and trucks in the ditch.

"I don't think it's wise for us to go farther than Sioux City," Hugh said, squinting into the opaque whiteness of snow swirling across the road in front of them.

Both Eugene and Ferne agreed at the time, but when they reached Sioux City it seemed that the storm was not quite as forceful as it had been. So they decided to go on to another town or two and see how things were. They crept forward, one icy, snow-covered mile after another. They were ahead of the storm, but they were afraid to stop for gas lest it catch them. Finally they reached Lincoln shortly after midnight, the blizzard close behind them.

Ferne cried in gratitude as she held their baby daughter, Diane, in her arms again. They were home safely in spite of the storm, and the children were well.

The old car had found the trip to Rochester and back as exhausting as it had been for the passengers. When they got it home, it once more coughed and rattled and smoked in ways that it never had before.

"I'm afraid it's going to quit on me," Ferne confided to Eugene. She did not like to concern him with such problems so soon after the serious operation, but she had to have his advice. "And we don't have the money to get it fixed."

"I know."

"Maybe I'd better take it to someone and see about repairs."

"At least you could find out what it will take to fix it."

She drove the tired old workhorse to one mechanic after another, but they all said that nothing short of a major overhaul would put it in shape again. Somehow it kept running the rest of the winter.

A short while after Eugene and Ferne returned from Rochester, Diane became sick. She had a terrible case of diarrhea that even a visit to the doctor did not seem to help. "This is just about it!" Ferne said in frustration. "Why should all of this happen to us? Haven't we had about enough for one family?"

Eugene turned quietly to her. "Why not us, Ferne?" he asked. "Who are we that we should receive special favor from God?"

2

"If You Ever See Again"

It was fortunate that as a boy Eugene learned to love the piano and enjoy practicing. His mother had decided, even before she was married, that her children would have piano lessons. So, when Eugene was in the fourth grade he was hauled to the home of a neighbor in North Platte, Nebraska, to start his musical education.

The gangling, rawboned lad took lessons for a few years before he started working on hymns at home after finishing his daily practice. It was not long after that that his uncle, who was in charge of junior church at the local Berean Fundamental Church, asked him to play for his services. The pastor, Ivan Olsen, says that Eugene was playing there when he was so small that he could not reach the pedals. Eugene does not think that is quite accurate, although he knows he did not look very big on the piano bench.

When Eugene was in the sixth grade, his dad called him into the living room one Sunday and made him a proposition. "If you'll memorize twenty-five songs well enough so you can accompany the congregational singing, Mother and I will buy you a bicycle." Every time Eugene went to town after that, he sought out the places that sold bicycles and longingly examined their stocks.

His parents helped him choose the twenty-five hymns he was to memorize and he set to work, going over the list, hour after hour. He had worked out his plan as he lay in bed at night, staring up at the ceiling. He was going to spend a certain amount of time on each new number, and when he had mastered it, he would move on to the next. He was determined that he would memorize those hymns quicker than even his parents thought he could, and then that wonderful bike would be his.

He had no idea how difficult it would be to memorize even one hymn, however. He had thought that because he had learned two or three bars of a song he played often, memorizing it all would be quite simple. But that was not the way it was. He would think he had a number memorized, but when he tried to play it through without music, he butchered it so badly that he began to get discouraged.

"You're having trouble," his mother told him, "because this is something you've never done before. The first two or three are going to be the hardest."

He soon learned that she was right. The first hymns were the most difficult to memorize. By the time he knew them he was developing a technique, and the task no longer seemed impossible. It was a proud day when he played the last hymn well enough so that his parents decreed that he had fulfilled his obligation and earned the new bicycle.

Eugene was in the sixth grade in 1937 when he believed in Christ as his Savior. Raised in a Christian home, he had gone along with his parents' faith in Christ without actually having committed his life to Him. Their church was having special meetings at one point that year, and every night he was hearing the plan of salvation spelled out. He was sitting at the piano at home one night during that week of meetings when he began to leaf through the invitatory hymns in the book he was using. The Holy Spirit used the words of the hymns to speak directly to his heart. He bowed his head and confessed to God his faith in Christ as his Savior.

Eugene was Sunday school pianist and had been riding his hard-won bike for a few years when he took another step along the road of preparation for the future. His parents and he learned of the Robert Harkness correspondence course for evangelistic piano playing, and he enrolled. The lessons proved to be a tremendous asset later, when he began to play the piano for Back to the Bible.

He was in high school when he began to accompany Pastor Olsen, playing the piano for his evangelistic services. The pastor used to challenge the crowd to call for a congregational hymn Eugene did not know. It got to be a game as the people tried to find songs he could not play. If they did succeed, he made sure that he learned to play that particular number before the next service.

Eugene's first recollection of doing anything creative musically came when he made an arrangement during his first year in senior high school. It was for a girls' trio to sing at a missionary conference that the fledgling Back to the Bible Broadcast was holding in Grand Island, Nebraska.*

Eugene wrote his first chorus the same year, sitting in the shade of a Chinese elm in his backyard. This was the golden era of choruses, and in a few years he sold eleven to Crawford, which were published in a booklet. He got three dollars apiece

*Back to the Bible Broadcast originated in Grand Island, Nebraska. Several years later Mr. Epp moved the organization to Lincoln, Nebraska.

19

for them and was so excited when the first was accepted that he stood on his head.

By the time he had reached his senior year, he had written a number of songs. Pastor Olsen had a little handwritten chorus book mimeographed and used as a giveaway item on the local radio program he conducted, even though Eugene had had no training in music theory and his feeble efforts broke most of the rules for good composition.

Eugene's acquaintance with Theodore Epp began as a result of their mutual interest in the fledgling Maranatha Bible Camp outside North Platte. Mr. Epp went there frequently, and Eugene played for many of the services that Mr. Epp attended or in which he spoke.

It was after one of those meetings that Mr. Epp approached him about playing for the Broadcast. "I'm honored even to have you think of me," Eugene said, "but I think I ought to finish high school and get some Bible-school training first."

"Oh," Mr. Epp replied, "you're still in school. You have to finish your education. Get your high school diploma and go on to Bible school. When you graduate, we'll talk."

Although Eugene was giving the Lord first claim on his piano, he was also active in secular music. He played the trombone in two high school bands, was in the school orchestra and a school trombone quartet, and sang in both the men's octet and the choir.

At the same time, he was active enough in sports to earn two major letters in basketball and three in track.

When Eugene graduated from high school, he enrolled at Wheaton College and went there the next fall. At the time the college did not have enough men's dormitory space, so he was assigned a room with an elderly Swedish couple who lived across town. They were a lovely couple and did their best to make him feel welcome, but he had never before been away from home for any extended period, and he was lonely and homesick. He could have made new friends, but he did not know how. He longed for a friend to talk to, someone to be with when classes were out or on Saturday when he had a little free time.

His discouragement took root and grew, compounded by the difficulty he was having with his course work. *What good does it do to study?* he asked himself. No matter how hard he tried, he could not get good grades. There was no use in deceiving himself. He was just barely passing. He was not college material. He crossed his little room as he thought about these things one day and pulled aside the curtain to stare out at the bleak, ice-covered street. Trying to make it in school was not worth what it was costing him. He was determined to serve God with his music. *Why, then, does God not help me with my studies?* he thought. *Why do I have to struggle so hard?*

During those agonizing days and weeks, he struggled with another, even more perplexing question. Lying awake at night, he would ask himself if there really is a God. What about all the sin and lack of love in the world—and the starvation, illness, and loneliness? If God is God, why did He create such an imperfect world?

Yet for all his doubting, in his heart he knew that there is a God and that He concerns Himself with the lives and problems of His children. Regardless of his grades and the other problems he had in college, regardless of what happened during the rest of his life, he had to believe that God is God and that Jesus Christ is His Son.

There was a mirror near the window. He faced it during one sleepless night, noting the dim outline of his own features in the semidarkness. *What about it, Gene Clark?* he asked himself. *Are you going to serve God or aren't you? If you are, you've got to forget this feeling sorry for yourself.*

From that moment on the matter was resolved. His doubting of God was gone and he no longer struggled with the temptation to leave school, even though the rest of the year was still difficult. He had to discipline himself to be independent and to overcome his loneliness. He also had to learn to study.

Spring broke early that year. It was wartime, and all the young men Eugene's age were drafted the summer before; but a sudden seige of arthritis in his feet and arms caused Eugene to be rejected. Toward fall the pain and swelling had subsided, and he was able to push thoughts of it into the hidden corners of his mind. It was almost forgotten until he began to have difficulty with his eyes.

He will never forget the first morning he noticed that something was wrong. He had been studying hard the night before and was later than usual getting up. The clock on the dresser indicated that he would have to hurry to get to his first class on time. Thankful that no one else was in the bathroom, he switched on the light and stood before the mirror, a glob of shaving cream in his hand. It was then that he saw the red film that had spread over the whites of both eyes. He moved closer and squinted into the mirror. *Strange,* he thought. He had never seen them like that before. And now that he saw there was something wrong, he realized that his eyes had been hurting him. The pain seemed to come from deep inside his eyes and radiate outward. He must have been studying harder than he thought.

His first tendency was to go on to class, but as he reached the campus he changed his mind and turned toward the Wheaton College health service

22

building. There was probably nothing wrong, he told himself, but it would not hurt to find out. The health service staff might be able to give him something to clear up the redness and ease the soreness.

Eugene was not alarmed, even when the doctor sent him to a local eye specialist. It seemed that there was a lot of fuss about a little problem that would surely correct itself in a few days. However, the specialist diagnosed his difficulty as iritis, an inflammation of the eyes caused by arthritis. He gave Eugene a king-sized injection of penicillin and referred him back to the college health service, where they put him to bed. Eugene was treated there for several days, but his condition worsened.

During one of the examinations a few days after Eugene first checked in, the doctor used a special instrument to look into Eugene's eyes. He frowned. It was obvious that he did not like what he saw. "I'd like your permission to give you an injection, Clark," the doctor said. "It will give you typhoid fever. You'll run a high temperature, which will kill the iritis."

Eugene's fever went so high with the injection that the doctor was frightened. He stayed in the room for a long while that night and finally got a nurse to take his place the next morning. He had indicated that there would be a series of typhoid shots, but that was the only one he gave.

For more than a week the doctor came to see the ill student regularly, but he did not seem able to slow the ravaging iritis. At last the doctor asked Eugene to go in to a Chicago hospital so that one of his former medical-school instructors could examine him.

The Sunday Eugene went in to the hospital was one of the most miserable days of his life. He lay on the bed in the strange hospital, wrapped in darkness and completely immersed in self-pity and homesickness. The next morning a young doctor examined him, and Eugene asked about how his eyes were doing.

"It will be some time until we know if you will ever see again," the doctor replied without thinking. Then he caught himself. "I—I mean until we—we know how long it will be until you're well and back in school again."

Eugene was stunned by the blunder. Not see again? He was preparing himself to serve the Lord in music. He had to have sight to read, compose, and do arranging. *Why has God deserted me?* he asked himself as he lay there, alone and dejected.

A few hours later the older doctor came in, confident and reassuring. Gently he told Eugene that he would watch his iritis closely and that everything would be all right. Thinking back later, Eugene realized that the specialist had actually not said anything to contradict what the younger man had so callously blurted, but there was something in his voice and manner that gave hope. Eugene began to relax and look forward confidently to the day when he would be well.

The following morning the specialist called in a number of other doctors for consultation. Eugene was given X-rays, sulfa drugs, and the then-expensive new drug, penicillin. And the doctors kept his eyes dilated. After ten days, his eyes began to clear.

As Eugene was released from the hospital, he realized that going back to school was impossible. By that time, the Wheaton College term was approaching the final exam period, and he had missed so much classwork that it would have been impossible for him to take the tests and do well in them. So he went back to North Platte, where he completed the year's work by correspondence. By fall he had perfect vision once more.

There were other problems that kept Eugene out of school the following year. His arthritis was so bad that studying was impossible, and he put in a painful winter that was punctuated by a trip to the warm springs of Excelsior Springs, Missouri, and the first visit to the Mayo Clinic in Rochester, Minnesota. There seemed to be no relief for him in either place, but with the coming of spring his arthritis began to ease. Once more he made plans to go back to school. This time he enrolled in the Moody Bible Institute.

Because he played the piano and organ, he got in on many special assignments at Moody. He was frequently called on to accompany soloists, quartets, and other small groups, in addition to instrumentalists. At the time he thought little about it, except that each invitation was another opportunity to serve Christ. Later he understood how God was training him for the day when he would be playing the organ for the world-wide Back to the Bible radio broadcast.

It was at Moody that Eugene came under the influence of some of the outstanding men in the world of Christian music. George Schuler was his piano and organ instructor. He took Eugene under his wing, explaining the intricacies of writing music and getting published.

Eugene was still having problems with iritis and arthritis from time to time, but he graduated from Moody Bible Institute and enrolled once more at Wheaton College. A severe flare-up of iritis forced him out of school a second time, midway in the 1949-50 term. He was home until the following fall, when he joined the staff of the Broadcast, the only other job he was ever to have. He will never forget the letter Mr. Epp wrote, asking him to join the staff. His first reaction was to write to Mr. Epp immediately, accepting the position. Yet, accepting the job could not just be Eugene Clark's idea. So he wrote Mr. Epp, thanking him and telling him that he would pray about it. He had to have the Lord's leading.

Several weeks later he got another encouraging letter from Mr. Epp. That settled the matter. Eugene took the job, rented an apartment, and moved to Lincoln. Neither Mr. Epp nor he thought to discuss the wages he was to get. He did not even know what he was earning until he had been working in Lincoln for two weeks and got his first check.

3

Those Wonderful Days

God had to have led Ferne Vincent, a petite, giddy, fun-loving redhead from Swanville, a small town in Minnesota, to a close walk with Him, Bible school, and eventually a job at Back to the Bible Broadcast. She was twelve years old when her mother, who had been widowed ten years before, managed to send her to camp at Medicine Lake, north of Minneapolis, where she was led to faith in Christ as her Savior. It was years later when she finally realized the significance of what had happened. She saw that she had been brought to Christ by a blind evangelist so that she could serve the Lord with Eugene, who was also to be blind.

With her new love for Christ, she had reached a pinnacle of joy and happiness there at Medicine Lake. The only thing more wonderful that could have happened to her right then would have been to have her Savior return and take her to be with Himself.

At camp she was sure she would always place Christ first in her life, but when she went back home she eventually grew cold and indifferent. And, as she entered high school, the rift between herself and Christ widened. Few of her friends even knew what it was to walk with Christ, and she was living very much the same as they were. Until midway in her senior year, no one could have known that she was a believer by the way she acted.

The group of friends Ferne spent her time with was clean and respectable, with a good reputation in school and the community. She tried to make herself believe that there was nothing wrong with the things she and her friends were doing if they continued to set high moral standards for themselves. However, it did concern her that few of her friends even knew she was a Christian. There were times at night when she was so overwhelmed by guilt that she could not sleep. Yet she could not bring herself to do anything about it.

Ferne cannot remember exactly what it was that first got her thinking about the spiritual mess in which she was living. It may have been a message at church or a casual remark by her mother, or it simply may have been the sobering fact that she was a senior and would soon be on her own. In any event, she finally saw that she had to quit compromising and commit her life to the Lord.

Her decision did not come easily. She fought against making it for weeks, trying to bargain with God to wait until after she graduated and went away to college. The friends she spent so much time with would be scattered, and those staying at home would soon have other interests. There would be little pressure on her to conform to her old ways. That would have been the easiest course of action, but God was not interested in making her decision painless. He continued to deal with her until finally she could resist no longer.

She could not have chosen a more difficult time to have made such a resolution. The junior-senior prom was imminent, and her steady boyfriend had already asked her for a date. Not knowing she was going to yield to the Lord, she had accepted his invitation. When she told him that she could not go to the dance with him, he was deeply disturbed.

"I don't get it," he said. "Don't you want to go with me?"

She tried desperately to make him understand, but when he saw that she had made up her mind, he stalked off. Their breaking up was big news in the little high school. Her newly expressed fanaticism, as her classmates called it, was an even bigger story, and for a few weeks her change of heart was the chief source of conversation in the halls.

Even though Ferne's fears of being ostracized were realized even more fully than she had anticipated, she soon discovered that it did not matter. God filled her heart and life so full that she had no room for loneliness or boredom. It had been several years since she had taken time for personal devotions. Now she could not get enough of the Bible.

The next fall she went to St. Paul Bible Institute. After graduation and a brief stint at Montgomery Ward's in the Twin Cities, she went down to Lincoln to work at Back to the Bible Broadcast. A year later Eugene accepted a position there.

They met shortly after he reached the capital city of Nebraska and started work. Then one day he had an attack of iritis and was hospitalized. Ferne and her roommate brought him a tiny fishbowl with two guppies they had raised.

It was not until several months after that that he asked her for a date. He had been going with another woman occasionally, but he was attracted by Ferne's thoughtfulness and happy smile. On their first date he took her to the midget car races. After that, he dated both women for six months before realizing that Ferne was the one for whom he really cared.

Even though he had never dated a great deal and

was thirty years old when he was married, he had done a lot of thinking about the sort of woman with whom he would one day share his life. He knew the importance of finding someone who shared both his love for Christ and his interest in music. Ferne had a deep, abiding faith in the Lord and, although her interest in music was not the same as Eugene's, she did appreciate it and knew a lot about it. As the months passed he felt drawn closer and closer to her.

He still did not know what he expected falling in love would be like; a bolt of lightning from a cloudless sky, perhaps, or a savage blow on the head. It was neither of those things. The realization that he was in love came slowly, a smile at a time. One day he just knew that Ferne was the girl for him.

They were both on the sentimental side. When he would be away for a few days with one of the Broadcast singing groups, she would always have a letter for him to open each day. He tried to do the same for her.

It was after returning from one of those trips that he told her he loved her. "I've gotten this far, Ferne," he said, frankly. "I don't want to string you along, and I know you don't want to do that with me. If you don't care for me, now is the time for us to break up."

Her eyes were moist as she tilted her head to kiss him. He did not remember what she said—or if she said anything at all—but he got the message.

Most young men find falling in love an exhilarating and joyous experience. For Eugene it was a time of indecision and trauma. There was no question in his mind but that he loved Ferne. But did he have any right to love her and expect her to marry him? He was having periodic attacks of iritis, and each carried with it the dread possibility of robbing him of his sight. Had he any right to expect a charming, vivacious young woman like Ferne to accept such a hazard?

He thought about composing a letter to her, explaining the situation and letting her know why he could no longer go out with her, but the very thought left him desolate. At that point, life without her would have seemed like an empty husk.

The other possibility was far more tempting. Marry her, if she would have him, and trust the Lord to take care of him and keep him seeing. She knew about his iritis and was well aware of his other health problems. If she was willing to run the risk, why should he hesitate? Unable to decide, he prayed for guidance.

The answer to his dilemma came at Thanksgiving in 1954. He decided to tell Ferne of his love for her and once more explain his health situation in minute detail. He would even insist that she go and see his doctor so that she would be fully aware of what the future might hold. Then, if she loved him enough to assume the risk, they would be engaged.

With that in mind, he asked her to go to North Platte with him to spend Thanksgiving with his parents. When the dinner was over and the dishes were done, he took Ferne to see some of the more interesting places around his hometown, and eventually he sought out the road to Maranatha Bible Camp. The sun was clinging to the rim of the western sky, throwing long, deepening shadows across the dry, crunching grass as he stopped and unlocked the camp gate with his dad's key.

They drove around the cottages, past the little lake, and eventually parked at the place where the dream of the camp first narrowed to a specific tract of ground. It was there that he took her in his arms and told her he loved her.

"I love you, too, Gene," she told him.

Then he had to tell her about his health. "I could go blind tonight, next month, or next year, or I might go on the way I am now for the rest of my life."

"God can intervene," she said, a quiet radiance spreading over her face. Her eyes were soft and a slight smile turned up the corners of her mouth. Gently she took his face in both hands. "I'd rather spend the rest of my life being your eyes," she went on, "than to be the wife of the wealthiest, most important man in the world."

He was lost in the exhilarating happiness that surged over him. She loved him and wanted to be his wife in spite of the threat to his future.

Eugene bought the ring for Ferne in December of that year, and toward spring he had to go to the Mayo Clinic with another attack of iritis and a new complication, glaucoma. Those were lonely times for him, especially the nights in the hotel, but he got a special-delivery, airmail letter from Ferne every day.

Their wedding was set for August 1, 1955. Eugene needed that much time to get ready financially for marriage. He had a little notebook with a list of the things he had to buy. Each month he checked off the items he had bought. First it was the tires, then the new clothes, and finally the money for the honeymoon. And by the time they were married they had made a down payment on a small house with a huge lot. The floors sloped, the doors sagged, and the aging windows rattled in the wind, but the owners of a mansion would not have been half as proud as they were.

Because most of their friends were in Lincoln, they decided to be married in the Central Christian and Missionary Alliance Church there, which they attended. They planned for a beautiful wedding, with three-tiered wooden candelabra in pink and white at every window in the church. Eugene worked for weeks making them. There were large candelabra for the front of the church and flowers and bows at every pew. When they finished, Ferne was satisfied that the church had never looked more beautiful.

They had not reckoned with the weather, however. Their wedding was on one of those scorching August evenings in a crowded church that was not air-conditioned. People were packed into every pew, and the latecomers were jammed at the back.

It was so hot that the dripless candles, which were supposed to be more impervious to heat than regular candles, had collapsed long before the ceremony was over. So did the cake that had been baked by Mrs. Ernest Lott and another of the Broadcast ladies. It sagged in places it shouldn't have and almost slid off the aluminum sheet it was on.

Pastor Ivan Olsen from North Platte married them, perspiration pouring down his face as he performed the ceremony. It was the same with Ferne's marimba students who played for the reception. They, too, looked as though they were going to collapse at any moment. People still remember their wedding as being held on the hottest night most of them could remember. "The thermometer stood at 108 degrees," one guest remembers.

They went to Estes Park, Colorado, on their honeymoon and then spent a few days with Eugene's uncle and aunt in Denver. From there they drove to Colorado Springs, where they stayed at a place with a little screened-in patio facing the mountains. They made a trip to Seven Sisters Falls at night in a torrential rain and a trip by car up Pikes Peak in a fog so thick that the ride was a terrible experience. The following afternoon they took the cog railway to the top of Manitou Mountain. The fog had given way to rain, but while they were on the slope the clouds began to drift away. On their way down, the sun broke through, forming the most gorgeous rainbow either had ever seen.

Ferne slid closer to Eugene and squeezed his arm. "Look," she whispered. To her it was more than a rainbow. It was a promise of a long and happy marriage that had God's blessing.

Returning to Lincoln, they settled into the little two-bedroom house they had bought the spring after they were engaged. It was almost falling apart, but they loved every loose board, every rotting sill, and every wind-leaking window. They had scrubbed or painted almost every inch of the entire house.

The work was particularly difficult for Eugene. It was not too long after he had had a severe iritis attack that they started work on the house, and his eyes were still foggy. He had a difficult time painting, but he insisted on keeping at it until the job was finished.

A month after they got back from their honeymoon, they began a ritual that they continued until they had three children and money was tight. They went out to a fancy restaurant for dinner once a month. When the children came along they still went out to eat at regular intervals, but the locale changed. Instead of the Cornhusker Hotel or Valentinos, they sought out a fast-food, hamburger restaurant. Still, it was a special occasion.

Ferne worked until a few weeks before Bruce was born in March 1957. She was more anxious than most prospective mothers and marked each passing day on the calendar. Ferne was not very large and weighed only eighty-seven pounds when they were married. The doctor said that she could have a five-pound baby by normal birth. A larger child would have to be delivered by Caesarean section. Eugene and Ferne were concerned about it and had been

34

praying about the matter for several months. At 12:30 one morning, she woke up with severe pains, and Bruce was born fifty minutes later, weighing five pounds, thirteen ounces. There were no complications.

After Bruce was born and they were wheeling Ferne down the hall to the maternity ward, she looked up at the doctor in his white outfit. Still drugged from the anesthetic and only dimly aware of what was going on, she said, slurring the words, "I know who you are. You're the Lone Ranger!"

When Bruce was scarcely able to walk, Eugene got him a baseball bat and took him out in the yard to teach him how to use it. He did not mention to Ferne his reasons for wanting to spend so much time with his son. Looking back, however, she realized that it was probably because of the precarious condition of his eyesight. He did not know how long he would be able to see to do things with his son, so he wanted to do everything with him while he could.

His iritis continued to give him difficulty, and the doctor started giving him cortisone. At the time, it was effective in controlling his arthritis.

Although Bruce was born without difficulty, there were problems with Bryan, who made his appearance in January, 1959. He was considerably larger at birth than Bruce. It was storming when they phoned the doctor to tell him Ferne was ready to give birth, and he told them to get right out to the hospital. When they got there, however, the woman in the admissions office refused to accept her. "We're completely filled," she said. "You can't have your baby here."

"But we called the doctor and he sent us here," Eugene said.

According to the woman, that made no difference. *She* was in charge of admissions.

"What are we supposed to do?" Eugene demanded, his temper rising. It was one of the few times Ferne had ever seen him disturbed.

"That's your problem," the woman said.

Eugene tried to phone Dr. McGinnis, who was in surgery at another hospital, but there was no way of getting in touch with him. He went back to the woman at the admissions desk. "Look at her!" he shouted. "We can't even get to another hospital. Get somebody here, and do it now!"

The woman phoned the head nurse, who grudgingly said that they should send Ferne to her, and she would try to find a place for her. A few minutes later a nurse almost as wide as the door stormed in with a wheelchair. Ferne flopped into it and was pushed into the laundry room, where they had put a bed.

Once they got her there, no one paid any attention to her, which disturbed Eugene more than ever. He stormed out into the hall, looking for someone in authority. He found their family doctor, who was also the chief physician at the hospital. He told him what had happened and expressed his concern.

Dr. Reed put on a white robe and had Eugene put one on. Together they went into the room, where Ferne was writhing in pain. He examined her without saying a great deal, told a nurse who came in to keep an eye on her, and went out. A few moments later the head nurse hurried in.

"I've never had such a tongue lashing in my life," she said. "Dr. Reed was really upset. He even called Dr. McGinnis out of surgery and talked to him." She timed Ferne's pains. "Are you a relative of Dr. Reed's or something?"

Bryan was born without incident. They did not name him after the hospital, Bryan Memorial, although they were accused of it.

4

Sunshine and Shadows

Eugene and Ferne lived in their honeymoon cottage until a short while before Bryan was born. They both loved the old house. The slanting floors of wide, slivered pine boards did not bother them, nor did the cold air and rain and snow that blew in around the doors. It did not even concern Ferne that the rooms were small and poorly arranged. She could cope with everything about the place except the mice.

They did not have regular mice like everyone else. There was so much open space around them that they had field mice. Eugene tried to convince her that they were cleaner than city mice, but she would not listen.

"To me, a mouse is a mouse," she said. "I know it's foolish of me, but I come completely unglued when there's a mouse around. They terrify me."

She might have been able to handle an occasional mouse, but the house was their convention center. All the mice in the neighborhood moved in. Eugene bought a box full of traps and set them all. As soon as he got home from work at night he would go from room to room, emptying traps and resetting them. In the morning he repeated the process. Ferne always said that if he had pelted those he caught, she could have had a coat of mouse fur.

The infestation got so bad that when they would return home after being away for the evening, he would go into the house ahead of her and turn on the lights, giving the mice an opportunity to scatter.

The summer before their first baby was born, Eugene and Ferne realized that they had to get another house. Their rooms were woefully small and so drafty that they were concerned about the new baby catching colds. And then there were the mice. The longer she and Eugene lived there, the more disturbed Ferne was by the continual invasion of rodents.

Together they prayed about getting another place. The house would have to be in a good neighborhood, they decided, so that it would hold its value. And it would have to be well designed, attractive, and solidly built. "I don't want to have to start repairing things before we get our stuff unpacked," Eugene said.

But there was another factor, even more important, since all the rest hinged on it. The price had to be one that they could afford. Salaries at the Broadcast were modest. Eugene and Ferne could not buy another house unless they could find one within their price range. "And," Ferne told him, "if we can't get something that suits our needs better than what we have, we might just as well stay where we are." He agreed with that.

Once they had decided to buy a house, they began to look, driving up and down the streets, phoning real estate agents, and studying the "houses for sale" section of the want ads. There were plenty of places for sale, but they could find nothing in their price range that seemed to fit their needs. They prayed about it regularly, but it seemed as though God was not listening.

Ferne had resigned herself to living in the little house and battling the mice, a resolve she kept until she and Eugene made the decision to buy something else. Then it seemed that her defenses shattered. The small rooms, the wide-board floors that were so difficult to keep clean, and the constant battle with mice overwhelmed her. She began to dread each hour in the house, and especially the nights when Eugene was away. Desperation seized her.

It was then that the Lord undertook for them. The place they finally settled on came up quite unexpectedly. Eugene saw it listed in the newspaper and phoned the real estate agent for an appointment to see it. On the way to the appointment he warned Ferne not to get her hopes up.

"I know," she said. Her voice was heavy and emotionless. "We've looked at *so* many houses in the last four or five months, and there's always something wrong with them. I'm beginning to think we'll never find anything different from what we have."

He reached over and laid a hand on her knee. He had to keep his spirits up to encourage her, but he felt the same. If a house they looked at was all right for them, the price was beyond reach. If the price was such that they could handle it, there was something wrong with the house that made it unsuitable.

As they neared the house, however, he had to agree that it was located in a good neighborhood. The homes were older, but there was evidence of a pride in ownership, and they were well cared for. "It doesn't look too bad from the outside, either," he said as he pulled to a stop in front and switched off the engine.

"We've been shown through houses like this before," she said. "And there's always some colossal drawback."

Eugene shrugged. "What have we got to lose?" he said.

The agent took them through the house. They went from room to room, expecting at any moment to find a crumbling basement wall, broken water pipes, or a faulty furnace or wiring. But the more they looked the more they were impressed. Everything was exactly as the seller had said it would be. They could scarcely believe it. They eagerly signed the papers.

But a problem developed. The owner, an elderly widower, decided that he did not really want to sell. The realty company that was handling the sale was quite disturbed and offered to find the Clarks another house in the same price range, but they had completely fallen in love with the one they had tried to buy. They prayed about it and talked it over. Eugene phoned the salesman and gave him their decision. "We'll wait until the house we looked at is available." That was the situation when Eugene went away for a week with the Broadcast quartet.

The mice must have been having a party in Eugene's and Ferne's bedroom during one night that Eugene was gone. There was a linen closet off the room that apparently served as the mice's town square; it seemed to Ferne that they congregated there by the dozens. Every time she turned off the lights, they would come running under the door and would scamper across the bedroom floor on tiny feet. She switched on the radio for company and the lights to keep the obnoxious little visitors out of the bedroom. At first she got Bruce up. She would keep him with her for a time, then put him back in his own bedroom, only to pick him up again. Finally she put him to bed and let him sleep. That proved to be one of the longest nights Ferne ever lived through. She was exhausted and completely shaken by the experience.

Before Eugene and the quartet got home from that trip, the real estate agent called. He could not understand it, he said. The owner of the house had been so firm in his decision to keep the house. Now he suddenly had decided to let the Clarks have it. He was going to stop in at the office in a day or two and sign the papers. Ferne was delirious with happiness.

When Eugene got back she told him everything that had happened, including her night of sleeplessness. But she had decided not to tell him anything about the other house unless he asked. It was not until they were in bed that he wanted to know if anything else exciting had happened while he was gone.

"No," she said, "not really—except that the real estate man called and said we could have the house."

He jerked himself upright. "What did you say?" he asked.

"We can have the house."

"Are you sure?"

"I'm sure that's what the man said."

Although they were going to move, there were some delays, and Ferne had one more terrifying incident with mice. Eugene called her from the office one afternoon, and she was so miserable and frightened that she was crying.

"There are mice all over the house!" she said.

"What are you doing now?" he asked.

"I'm sitting on the table." The tone in her voice warned him not to laugh.

"Where's Bruce?"

"He's sitting on the table with me."

It was then that he decided that if their new baby, who was due in a few weeks, was not going to look

41

like a mouse,* he had to do something. On the way home from work he stopped in a drugstore, explained the problem, and asked if there was something available that would work better than traps for getting rid of the mice. The clerk recommended a brand of poison, and Eugene bought an armload of it. In twenty-four hours the mice were gone. During the two months that they continued to live in the little house, they had no more problems.

But the damage was done. Every time Ferne walked into a room, she thought she could hear mice tiptoeing under the table, chairs, or the corner of the rug. No matter how angry she got at herself, no matter how much she told herself that the mice were gone and she had nothing to fear, she still panicked. She did not enjoy another day in that little house.

Eugene and Ferne had been married five years when he was invited to Denver for a lecture, recital, and seminar. He came home and told Ferne about the invitation. "Why don't you come along?" he asked her. "The folks will take care of the boys." By this time Eugene's parents had moved to Lincoln, and his dad was working at the Broadcast.

"What about money?" she asked.

"This is one thing I believe we ought to do whether we think we've got the money for it or not."

Eugene went out to Denver first, and Ferne came two days later. When he had finished teaching at the seminar, they headed for the mountains, going back to the same places they had visited on their honeymoon five years before. They ate in the same restaurants, wherever possible, made the same drives, and took the same walks.

God had decked the hills in all their blazing October splendor. Yellows, reds, and browns spangled

---

*An old wives' tale says that what a pregnant woman looks at might determine in part what her child will look like.

the greens of the forest; the sun seemed to smile just for them; and the stars and a pewter moon shone down from cloudless nights. It seemed to both of them that time had actually been suspended and they were back in the past, enjoying the first days of their lives together once more.

It was a memorable experience. As they headed back to Lincoln, Ferne snuggled in the crook of his arm. "Gene," she said softly, "this has been wonderful. I think we ought to plan to come back here again in another five years, just to renew our love for each other."

He agreed. It was something they would do every five years to bring back the memories of their honeymoon. Neither knew at the moment that that was the only time they would be able to do as she suggested. When their tenth anniversary came around, he would be blind and bedfast.

The summer before Diane, their daughter, was born, Eugene was having considerable trouble with his eyes. They took their vacation in Minnesota that year and, leaving the two boys with Ferne's mother, they went back to Rochester in the hope that something could be done to help him.

On the way they blew out two of their threadbare tires. That was problem enough, but the tires were an unusual size and there could have been a problem locating replacements. However, the first service station they stopped at had the size they needed, and the price was reasonable.

Word from Eugene's tests was far from encouraging. The doctors said there was little that could be done for him except to continue the treatment he had been using. Eugene and Ferne were disturbed when they got home, but they tried not to think or talk about it.

The following November, in 1961, Diane was born.

Ferne and the baby were still in the hospital when the specialist in Lincoln insisted that Eugene go to the Mayo Clinic immediately for surgery.

"I can wait until my wife and new baby get out of the hospital and we get our household settled down again, can't I?" Eugene asked.

"No, I want you to go as quickly as possible," the doctor said.

Fear stabbed deep into Eugene's heart as he sat in the examining room, thinking about the doctor's words. He thanked the doctor mechanically and left the room. His eyes were deteriorating, starting to bulge from the effects of iritis and glaucoma, and the doctor had determined that nothing short of an operation would stop it. This could be the dread moment they had been warning him about since he was a student at Wheaton College and he was examined in a Chicago hospital by the famed instructor. Other doctors on other occasions had told him the same thing. Now he was being urged to rush up to the Mayo Clinic.

His mind numb, Eugene left the doctor's office and made his way out into the brilliant early winter afternoon. The sun was warm and inviting, and the leafless trees swayed peacefully. There was a measure of hope in what the doctor proposed. The operation, if successful, could stop the ravages of iritis-induced glaucoma that threatened to rob him of his sight. But even as he expressed the possibilities for success, the doctor had explained the risks, which were great. The odds were against the success of the operation. It was entirely possible that the operation could leave him blind.

But the alternative, according to the specialist, was equally grim. If the operation was not attempted, he most surely would lose his sight. That was the bitter choice the doctor gave him.

Surely there had to be some mistake, Eugene

thought. He could not be in such a critical situation on such a day as this. He did not feel any different from the way he had when he went into the doctor's office an hour before to learn the results of the test. He could not be faced with making a choice that could result in his blindness. He had Ferne to take care of, and Bryan and Bruce and the darling cherub, Diane, whom the Lord had just given them.

And there were his duties at the Broadcast. Every year they got greater and more important and time-consuming. If he lost his sight he would be unable to continue. *Dear God,* he prayed, *You know how things are with me. I've got my family to take care of and my work at the Broadcast to do. Please spare my sight so I can support Ferne and the boys and Diane and continue to serve You.*

Standing on the walk and looking around, he examined his motives for praying that he be spared. He was concerned about his sight for personal reasons, he decided. To have denied as much would have been dishonest. But his chief desire was that he be able to care for his family and discharge his responsibilities at the Broadcast. He was glad that Ferne was in the hospital and that he would not be going up to see her until that evening after supper. It would give him a little time to get hold of his emotions.

Ferne and the baby were released from the hospital the next day. They went to the home of Eugene's parents, where it was decided that she would stay with the boys and the new baby while Eugene's dad took time off from work to drive him up to Rochester.

The morning they were to leave was cold and wintry, a typical late-November day. Ferne and Eugene stood at the front door while Hugh Clark got the car warmed up.

Bryan was still in bed and Bruce was running in

45

and out of the house, excited about what was happening. Eugene was having a difficult time controlling himself. The local specialist was sure that this time the doctors at the Mayo Clinic would operate, even though the chances of his being able to see after surgery were small. He might not see any of his little family again.

Ferne and Eugene were lingering at the door, finding it difficult to say good-bye but knowing that it had to come. Bruce came running up the front steps, his stocking cap pulled down over his ears to keep them warm. He looked up at his dad. "Don't worry about us," he said. "We're going to be all right."

When they got to the clinic and the examinations were completed, all the news was disturbing. The sight in one eye was completely gone. He only had partial sight in the other. The doctors completely disagreed with his Lincoln doctor, however. Although he needed the operation, the condition of his eyes had not stabilized, so they would not recommend surgery. They went even further. They refused to perform the operation at that time. Eugene thought he was prepared for any eventuality, but he discovered that he was not. Discouragement tore at him.

While Eugene and his father were in Rochester getting the discouraging news that the Mayo Clinic doctors would not operate on Eugene's eyes, Ferne discovered on a visit to their house that their furnace had gone out during a spell of sub-zero weather and that the plumbing had frozen.

Mrs. Clark, Eugene's mother, had been going with Ferne to check the house every two or three days, and they thought that that visit would be as uneventful as the others. As soon as they turned the key in the lock and stepped inside, however, they knew that they were in for trouble. The house was icy cold.

Ferne's first thought was for her plants. She had them all over the house. "Oh," she moaned, "my plants have all frozen."

She phoned Dr. G. Christian Weiss, director of missions at the Broadcast, who lived just up the street, and he lit the furnace. They waited, fearfully, as the heat came on, and it was not long before they discovered the extent of the damage. There was an indoor sprinkling system all over the house that came on as the ice in the aged pipes melted. Water poured from under the kitchen sink, in the bathrooms, both upstairs and down, and through the kitchen ceiling from the upstairs bathroom, bringing down the plaster. They had to replace all the plumbing in the basement and walls. New kitchen faucets and the toilet on the main floor had to be put in.

That night Eugene called and told her the bad news that the doctors had refused to operate. He would be coming home the next day.

She had not told him about the pipes being broken when he called, and she was concerned about telling him when he got home. He had been through so much during the past few days. Now he was returning to a house that was a disaster area. She did not tell him until they had eaten supper with his parents and he had played with the children for a while. When she finally told him about the pipes bursting, he took the news calmly, as he did everything else.

"Let's go over and take a look at it," he said.

He thought at first that Ferne was exaggerating the situation and that it was not as bad as she said. However, he soon learned that she had given an accurate picture of the damage. "But we've got good insurance," he told her. "I don't think we'll have any problems getting things back in order."

That proved to be the case. The insurance adjuster

replaced all the plumbing and put a new ceiling in the kitchen. That was the only ceiling in the house that had needed replacing before the flooding. They had often talked about taking care of it as soon as they got the money. Now they not only had new copper plumbing, but they also had a new ceiling in the kitchen. They concerned themselves with getting the work finished as soon as possible and were able to move back into the house the day before Christmas.

Holidays were always special at the Clark house. When birthdays came around, they always had a big cake and managed a few presents. Thanksgiving and New Year's Day were also big events, but Christmas was the grandest holiday of the year, especially after the children were born. They had never been able to spend a great deal of money on gifts, but they had never thought that that really mattered. The most important thing was the family's attitude toward the holiday.

That particular year they had so little money that they did not see how they could even buy a tree. That really upset Eugene. He had always had a tree at home when he was a child, and he wanted his own children to have one, too. On Christmas Eve, just before the stores closed, he went out to buy one. It was so late in the season that the store was giving the trees away. The one Eugene got was scraggly and poorly shaped, but to him it was the most beautiful tree he had ever seen.

With Bruce's and Bryan's eager but questionable help, they decorated the tree, sang Christmas carols, and told the story of Jesus' birth. When the children were finally in bed and asleep, Ferne came into Eugene's arms. "This has been a blessed time," she said.

He agreed with her. "But we sure didn't have much money to spend."

"We're together again as a family," she said. "That's all that counts."

They went into the living room and sat on the couch. "We've realized how quickly things can be taken from us," he said. "I think that makes us appreciate what we have a little more."

Their joy was short-lived, however. His eyesight continued to worsen, and his Lincoln doctor was still determined that he had to have surgery immediately. He sent Eugene to a specialist in Omaha, who gave him intensive tests and reached the same conclusion as the staff at the Mayo Clinic.

"I can't see doing surgery now," he said, "but I'm going to tell you something, son. You're in a burning building. Sooner or later, you're going to have to jump."

And that time did come, sooner than they allowed themselves to think it might. In June 1961, before their daughter was born, Eugene and Ferne went to the Mayo Clinic, only to be told that the specialists there would not perform the operation. In December of the same year, he and his dad went back, only to receive the same discouraging news. That was the time the pipes froze and broke, flooding the house.

A scant two months later, in February 1962 (the point where the story begins in chapter 1), at the urging of the Lincoln specialist, Eugene and Ferne went back to Rochester, where he was examined once more. This time the specialists' opinion was the same as that of his local doctor. Even though the risks were great that surgery might bring about the very blindness it was supposed to prevent, the operation had to be performed. If it was not done immediately, the loss of his sight was imminent.

After prayerful consideration, Eugene and Ferne signed the consent papers and he went into the hospital. Ferne had never experienced anything as traumatic as those torturously long days and nights following the operation. The success or failure of the surgery could not be known until the bandages were removed. She was in the room, tense and watching, while the doctor took the gauze from Eugene's eyes.

He can see! Ferne thought as Eugene walked over to Sallman's painting. *Praise God, he can see!* The operation had been a success. For a time, at least, his sight was preserved.

5

"Quick, Get the Doctor!"

Eugene could tell, as the months passed, that his eyes were getting worse. His condition deteriorated until the doctors at the Mayo Clinic, who had been reluctant to operate and on two previous occasions had refused, concluded that surgery was the only course left. They performed the operation and it was successful. He returned home, elated that he could see as well as he could; but he was aware of danger signals.

Each new attack of iritis blurred his vision and darkened the world around him. As it subsided he would begin to see better. The lights came on again and the fog began to lift. The outline of people and things, so vague and indistinct before, began to sharpen, and he would again be able to read and write. If he faced the truth, however, he had to admit that his sight never quite came back to where it had been before. Each attack seemed to steal something from his eyes, leaving him seeing less and less.

He did not try to hide that steady loss of vision from his wife. They had no secrets from each other. The truth was that neither would accept the fact that he was going to be blind. The next series of injections, the next visit to the specialist, or the new

51

medication the specialist prescribed was going to halt the weakening of Eugene's eyes. He gave only mental assent to the idea that he could go blind at any time. They prayed that God would save his sight and trusted Him to do so. There was never any doubt in the mind of either that Eugene was going to be spared.

It was during this period when he was having an iritis attack every few months that he began to think about writing a missionary cantata. He had always been interested in foreign missions and missionaries. Had his health been better, there was a good chance that he would have offered himself for Christian service overseas, so great was his burden for the people of Africa, the Orient, and South America. Through a cantata, he reasoned, he might be able to help challenge some young person to go or someone else to give.

So far as Eugene knew, no one had ever written a missionary cantata. He thought about it, prayed about it, and talked it over with Ferne. She thought it was a wonderful idea and urged him to talk to Mr. Epp about it.

"I can't do that," he replied quickly. "At least not yet." He thought the idea was good, but he did not have enough confidence in it or in his own ability to carry it out to tell anyone except his wife. "I want to get some work done on it first," he said. So he began to work evenings and weekends, setting songs on paper. After he had worked on the project enough to think that he could actually complete a cantata, he talked with Mr. Epp, Melvin Jones, and G. Christian Weiss. When he finished presenting the project and showing them what he had done already, Mr. Epp and Mr. Weiss glanced at each other. Then they turned to Mr. Jones.

"We think it's an excellent idea," Mr. Epp said, speaking for both of them.

Mr. Weiss' eyes twinkled. "Now, let's *all* get to work," he added. The look on his face changed the meaning of his words. "OK," he was saying. "You've got a good idea; now get with it, Eugene. You've got a lot to do."

That cantata, *The Greatest Story Yet Untold,* used many familiar hymns, along with a few new songs and various contemporary settings and things added to it. The use of the work of others lightened the load and helped Eugene to write and arrange the music for it. Without using the work of other composers, he is sure he would not have been able to complete the cantata. And, without what he learned in doing the first cantata, he knew he would never be able to write others. But he grew in knowledge and confidence, and when that cantata was published by the Broadcast and was well received, he was eager to start another.

When he suggested a second cantata, the men at the Broadcast were excited about the possibility. He had already decided that this one should be written along more classical lines. "I'm going after a heavier sound, Ferne," he said at home. "And I'm going to depend on the Scriptures for the lyrics, rather than poetry."

The work Eugene had set out for himself was such that it would tax the strength of a person with good health and normal eyesight. Looking back, he does not see how he was able to accomplish it. He never would have been able to write that quantity of difficult, original music had it not been that the Lord was giving him a strength and endurance far beyond himself.

He was just recovering from a bout with iritis when he started to search for a theme. Using a magnifying glass to read, he began to look through the New Testament for the message he wanted to get across. In Luke 24:44-48 he found it:

And he said unto them, These are the words which I spake unto you, while I was yet with you, that all things must be fulfilled, which were written in the law of Moses, and in the prophets, and in the psalms, concerning me. Then opened he their understanding, that they might understand the scriptures, and said unto them, Thus it is written, and thus it behoved Christ to suffer, and to rise from the dead the third day: and that repentance and remission of sins should be preached in his name among all nations, beginning at Jerusalem. And ye are witnesses of these things.

He was so excited that he was trembling. "Ferne!" he called out from the dining room, where he was sitting at the table with his Bible. "Ferne! I've found it! I've got the theme for the cantata!"

She came in from the kitchen and joined him, sitting in a chair across the table.

"I don't know why I didn't think of this before! I'm going to go through the books of Moses and the prophets," he said, "and find all the references I can about Christ and His purpose for coming into the world. I've even got a title: *Let the Earth Hear His Voice.*"

He saw the hurt in her face and misread it. "Don't you like the idea?" he asked, his own disappointment showing.

"Of course I do," she replied. "It's magnificent! Only—"

He knew then the source of her reluctance. She was thinking about his eyes and all the reading he would have to do to search the Scriptures for verses to set to music. "If it's too hard for me to read," he told her, "the Bible is on long-play records. I can get a set and *listen* to the verses I'll need."

Her face brightened. "And I'll help do what I can."

Although he appreciated her offer to help far more than he could ever tell her, her trying to help did not prove to be too practical. He was doing most of the work at the office, and with three children to care for, Ferne was tied to their home.

He soon realized that she was right in being concerned about his ability to read so much. He had to resort to the recordings of the Bible. Sitting at his desk and listening to the Scriptures hour after hour was tedious. He would know approximately where a verse was located in the Bible and could have found it quickly with the help of a concordance if he had been able to see well enough to read. However, finding a specific verse on a long-playing record was both exasperating and time-consuming. There were days when it seemed that he had accomplished nothing, and he would come home at night completely frustrated.

"If only I had memorized more Scripture," he complained to Ferne.

"You'll get it," she said confidently. "It may take you a little longer than you've planned on, but you'll get it." Never once did she doubt that the cantata would be completed or that it would be a big success.

Eugene needed that assurance. The task was so great and the difficulties so hard to overcome that he might not have continued until the project was completed without Ferne's calm confidence. When he would come home after a particularly trying day, she had just what he needed to lift his spirits and give him the drive to get back to work the next morning.

The people at the Broadcast were also helpful. They provided for him a typewriter with huge type so that he could read what he had written. And Ferne's former boss, Glenn Jones, had the printing department prepare staff paper with lines an inch apart. The entire staff was six inches high. Eugene used a large grease pencil to set his music to paper.

There were times during the period when he was working on the cantata that his sight was a bit more clear than normal. When that happened he wrote furiously, trying to get as much on paper as possible before the clouds came again. Finally he got it written and rewritten. When he checked in the flags and dots and measure bars, he had to use a small magnifying glass, which made the process slower than normal. At last, however, it was finished. He had completed the most difficult musical task he had ever undertaken.

This was during the period when the Broadcast was making six programs a week and he was playing every day, That meant he had thirty-five songs to play each week, and often he had to do new arrangements for them. His eyesight deteriorated so badly that year that much of the time he had great difficulty seeing. He could just make out Pop Bennet's arms as he raised them to start or stop the music.

After he had done the new arrangements, he would practice them with a magnifying glass until he had memorized them. Only then did he trust himself to play them for the programs. Still, he did not think he should sit down at the organ without sheet music. He was concerned that it would shake up Pop, the director, and the people in the choir. He could imagine how much confidence they would have in him if they knew he was playing without music. He had never seen anyone in music who did not have an occasional memory lapse, when everything would flee the mind. It was against such occurrences that many excellent musicians always had the music at hand. For that reason he carried his music down to the organ every day and arranged it on the rack in front of him.

It was not his intention to deceive anyone. He was

concerned only with the mental well-being and the confidence of the choir. He wanted them to be able to concentrate on their singing without having to worry about their accompanist and when he was going to make a mistake.

They were practicing one morning when Ernest Lott came up and stood behind him. Eugene knew someone was there, of course, but he was not aware of who it was. It really did not bother him. It was the sort of thing that happened occasionally. When he finished there was a brief silence. Then Ernest spoke.

"Eugene," he said quietly, "you're playing from memory, aren't you?"

Eugene turned on the bench and looked up at him. Mr. Lott's face was a blur. "Yes," he said simply. There was no purpose in making any alibis or explanations. Mr. Lott had asked a direct question. He deserved a direct answer.

"I thought so," Mr. Lott said. "You've got your music upside down."

Eugene wondered afterward if that would make any difference in his relationship with the Broadcast, but it did not.

He had another problem that he tried to keep from everyone at work. It was such a little thing that, when it was resolved, he wondered why he had cared whether it was known. The problem was that he had difficulty finding the steps at the back of the hallway that led to the studio. He was not aware that anyone even knew about it until he went down to practice one morning and saw that a small light had been installed over the door to help him locate the steps and negotiate them.

The glaucoma that was also affecting his sight was slow acting. At times it would flare up—usually during an iritis attack—and he would be unable to see more than the dim outline of things around him.

Then it would get better, and for a time he would be able to see quite well again.

Even though his sight was slowly deteriorating, there were no serious health problems during the entire year. Then in June 1963 disaster struck. Neither Eugene nor Ferne had thought anything about it when he came home from work with the flu one day. He did not seem to be very ill. He sat with the rest of the family at the table and ate a little supper, but afterward he excused himself.

"I don't feel very well," he said. "I think I'll go up to bed."

About an hour later he was sick to his stomach and vomited. They were both so naive that they thought little about it, even though the vomit was bright red. They attributed the color to the red gelatin dessert he had eaten for supper.

Ferne does not know why she phoned a nurse friend who lived two blocks away and asked her to come over. She certainly had not felt concerned enough about Eugene to do so. God must have directed her in her ignorance, because the situation was critical. The nurse came in, checked his pulse and blood pressure, and went immediately to the bathroom to look at the vomit in the toilet bowl. Ferne saw her face blanch.

"We'd better call the doctor," she said, trying to stay calm.

Ferne went to the downstairs phone and called Dr. Reed's office, and the nurse talked to the doctor. By the time the conversation was over, the nurse was in full control of herself. "The doctor is going to call the hospital and have them get ready for Eugene," she said crisply. "And he'll send an ambulance."

Ferne felt the strength leave her knees. Her friend's quiet statement had confirmed what she was beginning to suspect—something terrible had happened.

6

"We're Doing Everything We Can for You"

Ferne moved through the house with her mind in a haze, as if in a dream. She knew what was happening, but it was as though it was happening to someone else and not herself. She was completely detached from reality as she watched her friend check Eugene's pulse and blood pressure. It was a play on television that would soon be interrupted by commercials; a terrible dream that would wake her up before long and she would be so shaken that she would not sleep the rest of the night. In her heart, however, she knew that it was none of those things. There was no fantasy in the pallid lifelessness of Eugene's face or the fear in her friend's eyes and voice. Slowly she began to realize that something terrible was happening.

All of a sudden she wanted to cry, but she could not. The fear, bewilderment, and hurt were so deep that she was beyond crying. She could not even pray. In her anguish she could not give voice to the torment of her heart. Yet, strangely, there rose up within her a great, agonizing, wordless cry for help. She could not form words, yet every breath, every movement, every tense beat of her heart was a prayer.

As soon as Eugene learned that he had to go to the hospital, he decided to shave. When no one else was in the room he got his electric razor and turned it on. At the first whir the nurse gave a cry of alarm, flew up the stairs and burst into the bedroom.

"Eugene Clark!" she shouted. "Stop shaving this instant! Lie back down and be perfectly still! You're not to finish shaving or do anything!"

Ferne left the children with her friend and rode to the hospital with Eugene in the ambulance. Dr. Reed met them, had Eugene placed in intensive care, and checked him thoroughly. His condition seemed to stabilize during the night, but Ferne could see that the doctor was still as concerned as ever.

"We'll have to run some tests in the morning," he said, "to find out exactly what's going on."

She did not know it then, but Dr. Reed had also ordered blood of Eugene's type and had a transfusion set up just outside the door in case it was needed in a hurry. She relaxed a bit, but an empty, sickening feeling still gripped her. She lay down for a little while but could not sleep. Every time she closed her eyes she could see her husband lying there on the gleaming white bed, pale and motionless.

The next morning Dr. Reed came in and examined Eugene once more. He had just left when Eugene turned on his side and raised himself on one elbow. Before Ferne could say anything he vomited blood all over her and the bed. It gushed out in one awful flood. Then his eyes rolled back in his head and he sank back on the pillow, unconscious.

Ferne must have screamed, although later she could not remember that she had. A nurse came running in, and Dr. Reed was not far behind. They worked frantically over him while Ferne stood motionless, immobilized by terror.

Eugene regained consciousness briefly. He opened his eyes and looked up into the kindly face of the man bending over him. "Son," he heard Dr. Reed say, "we're doing everything we can for you!"

In a few moments Ferne became aware that they had wheeled the transfusion apparatus beside the bed and were trying to get needles for blood and intravenous solutions into his veins, but without success. "I can't seem to do it, doctor," she heard the nurse say. The nurse's voice sounded as though it were coming from some far distant place, drifting down a long, hollow tube. "His veins have collapsed."

The nurse tried again without being able to do it, and Dr. Reed called for one of the male attendants who was particularly adept at inserting the big needles. He came as soon as he was paged, and in a few moments he was able to find the veins and get the transfusion and the intravenous medication started.

Eugene was conscious for a time after the doctor spoke to him. He was aware that they were giving him oxygen and that the intravenous medication and blood transfusion were going. Then he blacked out again and did not regain consciousness until late evening, when he came to enough to hear voices outside the door. He would have recognized one speaker's voice anywhere. It was the voice of Melvin Jones, who was talking to Ferne. Eugene closed his eyes, smiling slightly. Everything was going to be all right, he decided. People were concerned and praying.

As the blood poured into his frail body day by day, he came out of shock and regained consciousness. He was still very ill, but the transfusions began to give him strength. It was slow, but Ferne could see a little progress every day. Still, it was a week before he was far enough along the road to recovery to be x-rayed and to take the other tests that the doctor ordered.

Dr. Reed was not optimistic from the first, but he did not talk to Ferne about the cause of Eugene's sudden hemorrhaging until the tests were completed. "We just don't have enough information yet to determine the cause of the trouble," he would say when she asked him.

She would look up at him, trying desperately to keep her voice steady. She still felt as though she was in some horrible nightmare. "You will let me know as soon as you find out, won't you?" she would ask. Then he would nod somberly.

All along, the doctor's attitude revealed that he was expecting the worst, but Ferne was completely unprepared for the bombshell he dropped on her when the tests were finished. She continued to assure herself that it did not matter what the X-rays showed. God had brought Eugene through this ordeal. He was going to undertake for him. Somehow, at some time in the future, He was going to heal her husband so that he could keep on working and taking care of his family.

After the tests were finished, Dr. Reed called Ferne into his office and had her sit down. She could tell by the concern on his face that he had bad news. "I'm sorry to have to tell you this, Ferne," he said as gently as possible. "The tests indicate that there are a number of things wrong with Eugene in addition to his iritis and arthritis. There is a kidney problem, but we have consulted with a specialist who feels that Eugene is too weak for him to do the necessary tests—

She waited expectantly. There was more to come. She knew that. She had been around Dr. Reed enough to know something about his manner.

"But, there is more," he went on. "There is every

indication that Eugene has cancer."

Cancer! she thought. She went numb. Her eyes glazed and a wave of nausea engulfed her. She thought she was going to be sick right in the doctor's office. In her worst fears she had never imagined anything so terrible.

No! she protested inwardly to God. *Eugene has gone through enough! He has suffered for years with iritis, glaucoma, and arthritis. He can't have anything else wrong with him. It isn't fair!*

"Are you sure?" she asked, speaking aloud. Her voice sounded dull and strangely detached from her body.

"No," he acknowledged. "We are not positive. We can't be until we do surgery and a biopsy, but it is my considered opinion, based on the extensive tests we have taken, that we are dealing with cancer."

She does not recall leaving Dr. Reed's office or going in to see Eugene afterward. She does not even remember going home from the hospital. Mercifully, God blanked out those awful hours, as though they had not happened. She had some arguments with the Lord in the days that followed.

Why should one person have to suffer so much? she asked. All his adult life Eugene had been forced to bear so many health problems. It was not fair that he would also have something like this to face. *If these things were happening to someone like me,* she reasoned, *it would be a little different. I really am not doing much for God, and I know my own weaknesses—my frailties. But Eugene has long placed God first in everything and is a faithful servant.*

"They need him at the Broadcast, God," she said aloud. "His work there isn't finished. And it isn't finished at home, either. The children are still so small, and they need him so very much."

She did not mention herself or her own need of her

husband. Somehow that seemed selfish to her. But there were so many others who depended so much on him that she could not see the justice in God's taking him home.

She reminded God of the sort of life Eugene had lived since he was small and of the unselfish way in which he had used his talent to help bring people to Christ. As she pleaded and argued with God, her heart crying out in prayer every waking moment, she expected an answer. But there was none. The heavens seemed closed against her, and she was bewildered and hurt. Never before had she felt so desolate and helpless, so alone.

Eugene had a more complete victory over fear, even during those dark hours, than his wife, but there were times of deep concern. Hour after hour he lay in the hospital room, staring up at the ceiling. There had been a time—years ago, it seemed—when Ferne voiced that age-old cry of bewilderment and pain at all the trouble that engulfed them. "Why us, Lord? Why? *Why?*"

He could hear himself replying, "Why not us, Ferne? Who are we to expect more favorable treatment from the Lord?"

At the time he had believed what he said. He thought he still believed it, but it was much more difficult now. He had been ill before and the threat of more serious trouble had hung over him, and there were the problems with their old car and a lack of money to repair it. Still, they were able to continue living very much as they had in the past. Now, however, they were facing an uncertainty they had never faced before. He might be taken from his little family that needed him so much, and from his work at the Broadcast. It was not so easy to say "Why not us?" under such circumstances.

He prayed, asking God for strength and courage and, if it was His will, healing. He also prayed for his wife and children, asking God to give them strength to face the future and to take care of them, whatever happened.

Dr. Reed and the men he called in for consultation decided that Eugene must go through an operation. During those few days before surgery, Ferne prayed that God would help her to keep her own fears and concern from showing through. She smiled brightly as she would enter his room and talk about the things they were going to do when he was released from the hospital. She hoped that they would be able to go out to North Platte to Maranatha Bible Camp before the summer sessions ended, she said, even though they probably could stay only for a few days. If the doctor would allow him to make the trip, she thought they should go. She was sure he would recover much quicker there.

She spoke confidently, but on the inside she felt dead and cold, as lifeless as straw from the combine after harvest. As she sat in the hospital room, chattering about the kids and herself and the things they were going to do when he was on his feet again, she wondered if she was lying in her forced gaiety. She had been careful not to say anything to him that was actually untrue, but she wondered if her attitude—her false cheerfulness—could be considered a lie. She certainly was experiencing none of the joy she was trying so hard to show.

Eugene talked about how much stronger he felt and how glad he would be when the operation was behind him. He had a great deal of work at the office to do and he should be getting back to it as quickly as possible, he said. It was hard to catch up if one got too far behind.

Neither Eugene nor Ferne was aware that Dr. Reed had talked to the other about the strong possibility that he had cancer. Ferne was trying to act as though he was getting better every day and

65

the operation he faced was only routine. Eugene was trying to make her believe that the surgery was the sort of thing he went through every day and that there was no cause for concern.

They both knew, however, that the operation was far from routine. And if they had not known, they would have learned it a day or two before the surgery was scheduled, when the doctor took the unusual step of allowing Eugene to see the boys. Diane was so small that Dr. Reed did not think it wise for Ferne to bring her. But Ferne brought the boys into the hospital by the back door, put Eugene in a wheelchair, and took him out into the hallway to spend some time with them. He talked with them for a few minutes and gave them each fifty cents to spend on fireworks.

The night before his surgery, the nurse forgot to give Eugene his sleeping pills; but the Lord had given him such peace about the coming operation that he slept very well. Early that morning he got up and washed and shaved. He was ready and waiting for the orderlies when they came in to prepare him for surgery.

After the operation, the first thing he recalled upon coming out from under the anesthetic was seeing a semicircle of nurses and nurses' aides around his bed. There must have been six or seven of them. That was when the doctors made the pronouncement that there was no malignancy. His mind was so woozy that he could think only that those nurses were a cheering section for him.

When the operation was over and the doctors' tentative diagnosis of cancer was proved wrong, Eugene and Ferne confessed to each other their attempts at deception. "I wanted to spare you the worry and concern if I could, Ferne," he said softly. "I didn't want you to get upset until we knew for sure."

"And I didn't want to worry you," she said. "I didn't know what Dr. Reed had told you, but it doesn't really matter. It was just a stomach ulcer caused by all the cortisone that you've been taking."

Although they knew the surgeon had removed a third of Eugene's stomach, they did not realize the full import of the findings or how they were going to affect his physical condition in the future. They were so thankful he did not have cancer that they did not fully consider the meaning of the ulcer.

When Eugene got home from the hospital, he and Ferne talked with the children about his physical condition. They did not try to tell them things they were too young to understand, but in general terms they tried to explain that their daddy was sick and that the time might come when he would not be able to see. Talking to them was Eugene's idea. He wanted them prepared in case he did go blind.

When he first came home from the hospital after the operation, he spent most of his time in bed. Diane was little then, so tiny that it was hard for her to crawl up on the bed to be with him.

"Let's talk, Daddy," she would say, or, "Let's tell stories." She loved to have him tell her stories.

On one occasion when she was in bed with him, he turned his head enough so that she was able to look through the thick left lens of his glasses. Her eyes widened in surprise.

"I think I know what your problem is, Daddy," she exclaimed. "I couldn't see through those glasses, either."

Ferne laughed along with Eugene, but inside she was crying. And that night when she was alone after the children had gone to bed, the tears came freely, soaking the pillow. It hurt so much to see him that way.

After a time Eugene was able to go back to work, but he was having a great deal of trouble with his eyes. He was still memorizing his music at the studio and was able to do his arranging and composing only with great difficulty. During this period Ferne cried a lot when she was alone. It all seemed so unfair. She saw Christians all around them who were proud and arrogant and materialistic. They could not even approach Eugene's spiritual depth and devotion, yet they were getting along beautifully. *This doesn't make sense, Lord!* she would tell God. *Eugene is so committed to you, and here he is going through all of this!*

Those were difficult days for her. She prayed continually that her husband's sight would be restored, growing so desperate that she demanded that God heal him. *This is it,* she would pray. *This has gone on long enough. Tomorrow Eugene is going to see!* Ferne had been a believer for many years and had long considered herself a mature, dedicated Christian, but there was so much she had to learn about God and prayer, so much she had to discover about the Christian life and the tribulation that is visited on some.

The day finally came when she realized that God does not reward believers for their love and devotion to Him—on this earth. As Eugene had to tell her many times, "This is our ministry, with our lives and health just as they are. He has entrusted to us a special kind of ministry now. It is up to us to make the most of it."

Slowly she began to see life as a challenge, as an exciting adventure. It was not a giving in or giving up. All along they both continued to expect something to happen. Maybe the medicine would work. Maybe surgery would restore his sight. Perhaps some scientist, working somewhere on the problem right then, would come up with a new treatment that would take care of this sort of problem. Perhaps God would miraculously heal Eugene's body. They did not give up but instead looked forward confidently toward each new day in the assurance that God would give them what was best for them for that day.

Someone sent them a copy of *Living Letters* (the first volume of the work that became *The Living Bible*). They found a verse in it that meant a great deal to them. It helped Ferne, particularly, when people who came to visit Eugene would say, "Brother, we don't understand it here, but you hang on and some day it will be better." She knew they were trying to be helpful, but she did not want to hang on for the next forty years. She wanted victory in Jesus Christ right then. And that was what this verse promised:

When we have trouble or calamity, when we are hunted down or destroyed, is it because he doesn't love us anymore? And if we are hungry, or penniless, or in danger, or threatened with death, has God deserted us? ... but despite all this, overwhelming victory is ours through Christ who loved us enough to die for us (Romans 8:35, 37, TLB).

Eugene and Ferne spent much time searching out the Scriptures, both together and in their private devotions. He would listen to his recordings of the Bible over and over again when his sight was too bad for him to read, and something would impress him. She occasionally came across a verse or a portion in her own reading that was challenging or helpful. And sometimes they found a helpful passage when they were reading the Bible aloud together.

This was a time of growing, especially for Ferne. She was learning more about trusting Christ. Later, she understood that God spoke to her in many ways during those months to prepare her for the difficult road ahead.

7

"This Is the End of Your Eyes"

Although Eugene was back at the Broadcast working part-time by early fall after his stomach surgery, he was not making the progress he should have. Dr. Reed did not say much to either him or Ferne about it, but they could tell that he was not satisfied with the way things were going. Eugene tired more easily than before, and his eyesight was deteriorating. Eugene was aware of both symptoms but tried to avoid the thought that they indicated more trouble to come. Eugene told Ferne that he was sure the problems were caused by the operation and that he would be himself in a few months.

However, Eugene's health difficulties seemed to climax in early November 1963 with a severe attack of iritis. "I'm going to have to have you take me to the specialist, Ferne," he said when he got up that morning and realized that he could not see enough to take a single step without assistance. He tried to keep her from sensing his concern, but he did not succeed.

They drove down to the doctor's office, and Ferne helped Eugene get out of the car and make his way through the door and up the steps. They had both been through similar experiences—enough to keep them from being panic-stricken when an iritis attack came—but he was aware that this one was different. It hit with an intensity that could not be denied.

It was difficult for him to know why he was aware that this attack was more serious than the others. He had occasionally endured pain that was as harsh as it was this particular morning, and he had been left in darkness before. Perhaps the darkness that surrounded him now was a bit more completely devoid of light than that in other episodes. Perhaps he only sensed the difference. Whatever the reason for it, he seemed to know that his eyes were definitely worse. Yet he was not prepared for what the doctor told them. Neither was Ferne. The specialist examined him carefully and for a minute was silent.

"This is the end of your eyes, Eugene," he finally said with a coldness that they were sure he did not feel. "I would strongly suggest that you get in touch with the group for the blind and start making application for reading material and other things that they can provide to help you."

To Ferne, his statement was like a kick in the stomach. Eugene could not see her reaction, but he also shuddered and reeled under the blow. Although there had been hints that his problem was more severe this time, they had been expecting nothing like that.

"Is there anything we can do?" Ferne asked him weakly.

"There isn't anything anyone can do," he replied. "We have known for a number of years that one day this was going to happen. Now it has."

Neither Ferne nor Eugene said much on the way home. There are times when words are empty and meaningless. Ferne was thinking about him, and he was thinking about her and the kids, wondering how he was going to take care of them. They had tried to be frugal, but with his illness and all the expenses it caused, they had no savings. He remembered hearing Ferne tell what a difficult time her mother and sister had after her dad died. This would be even worse from a financial standpoint. He did not see how he would be able to make any financial contribution to the care of his family, and yet his costs would continue.

Eugene was as discouraged that morning as he had ever been. Always before he had been able to see how God would work things out. This time he was so crushed by the news that he could not understand how the problems could be solved. He had read verses in the Bible that told him God would give him strength to stand whatever happened, and another verse said that all things work together for good. He tried to quote Romans 8:28, but he was so distraught that he could remember only the first few words. He prayed silently, but there was little comfort or help for him.

As soon as they got home from the doctor's office, Ferne phoned the Broadcast and told the people there what had happened. They called a special chapel to pray for him.

Miraculously, the next morning when Eugene woke up he could see—not very well, but he could make out the shapes of the chair across the room and even the tree outside the window.

"Ferne!" he cried. "Ferne!"

Frightened, she came running up the stairs and into the bedroom.

"I can see! I can see!" he shouted.

He could not see the tears of gratitude and joy that were streaming down her cheeks, but he knew her so well that he *knew* they were there.

Although a measure of Eugene's sight had returned that morning, he could not see well enough to drive, so Ferne took him down to the specialist's office. He went in alone, and the doctor stared incredulously at him.

"I don't understand it," he said, shaking his head. "Humanly speaking, you have no right to be seeing at all."

Eugene did not say anything to him, but he was very much aware that God was not ready for him to be sightless just yet.

For an entire week they rejoiced over that tremendous victory. Then the bomb exploded again, with devastating results. Eugene had gone to the office on Monday and had worked all week. On Friday night he stayed at his desk until six o'clock. He and Ferne were going out to eat, and he was planning to return to the office to finish the manuscript he had been working on. They had a wonderful time that night; such a wonderful time that he did not get back to his desk as he had wanted to.

"I left my pencil and manuscript and everything out," he told Ferne as they turned in at their drive. "I guess I'll have to go down in the morning and work for a while." But he didn't. He did not know it at the time, but he was never to go back to his desk.

Saturday morning when he got up, he did not feel like going to the office. He could not say that he felt ill. It was just that he had a sharp pain in the pit of his stomach that would not go away and a leaden heaviness that he had never known before. He did not think a great deal about it. It was just that he did not think he was up to going back to work that morning.

When Eugene left the hospital after the ulcer surgery, Dr. Reed had suggested that he keep a vacuum bottle of milk at his bed so he could have a glass during the night. On Sunday evening he took his bottle of milk and went to bed. He had not been there long before he hemorrhaged again.

The instant Ferne realized what was happening,

she called Ernest Lott. She does not know why she called him, except that he and his wife, Annie, were two of their best friends. Actually, they had been Eugene's friends before they even knew her. He had lived with them before he and Ferne were married.

Ernest lived half a mile from them, but it seemed that he was at their house in about the same length of time that it took Ferne to hang up the phone and get back to the bedroom. He also hurried to the bedroom. He saw that Eugene was vomiting blood, and fear filled his kindly eyes.

"We've got to get you to the hospital, Gene," he said, trying hard not to let his concern be seen by either of them. "I think I can help you down the stairs and out to my car."

Ernest was so frightened that all he could think about was getting Eugene to the hospital as quickly as possible. However, he realized that Eugene was too ill to make the trip by car, so he phoned the police. They got an ambulance to the house in what seemed like record time. Both Ernest and Ferne thought Eugene would bleed to death before they got him to the hospital.

They were almost ready to leave when Pastor Curt Lehman came to the house. Ferne did not know then how he found out about Eugene's sudden hemorrhage, but he met them on the front porch as they were on their way to the hospital. He was a great encouragement to her in the days that followed, but at the moment she was so overwrought that she was only dimly aware of his presence.

Dr. Reed was at the hospital when Eugene was wheeled into intensive care, and he started transfusing blood into him. Ferne sat there, watching in horror, as they forced the blood into his frail body through a needle in his arm and took it out through a tube that ran down his nose and into his stomach. For five days and nights she stayed in his room, sleeping a bit now and then in the straight-backed chair beside his bed but never leaving him for more than a few moments at a time.

Kay Roberts, who worked at the Broadcast, came up to the hospital with hot coffee for her every morning. Ferne supposed someone brought her a sandwich or a little other food from time to time. She does not remember much about that, except that she did not go out to eat.

"You'd better go and have something to eat and a little rest," one of the nurses told her.

She shook her head. Eugene was lying there in shock and unconscious, but he might open his eyes, if only for a moment. When that happened she wanted to be there—to let him know that she was in the room.

During those awful hours, she learned much about trusting completely in the Lord. She kept praying, "Lord, help me make it until noon.... Help me make it until supper.... Help me make it until morning."

This time she did not complain bitterly to God for what was happening. Instead, she thanked Him, honestly, for being with her—with her and Eugene. She reveled in the strength that could come only from Him.

She cannot say that those hours were easy. They were probably the most difficult she had ever experienced until then. Yet, there was peace in her heart. She felt the love of God all around her. Had it not been for those five long days and nights alone in the hospital room with Eugene and God, she would have come completely apart when, a few weeks later, he lost his sight and arthritis twisted his sensitive, talented fingers to uselessness. It was the time in that hospital room that forged the steel in her soul so that she could face the trials to come.

Eugene's memory of those days in the hospital is

sketchy. He drifted in and out of consciousness, aware that he was in the hospital and very ill. He felt the needle in his arm when he tried to move, and he knew that Ferne was in the room. However, he was too sick even to be concerned about her.

Late one evening he regained consciousness for a few moments as the doctor bent over him. "Squeeze that transfusion as hard as you can!" he heard the doctor say to the nurse beside him. "We've got to get more blood into this fellow!"

Not long after that he woke up just long enough to talk to Ferne for a few minutes before they wheeled him into surgery.

Ferne wondered how Pastor Lehman first came to be interested in Eugene and herself. They were not members of his church. It could have been that he knew of the Clark family's connection with the Berean Fundamental Church in North Platte and that Pastor Ivan Olsen would have been with them had he lived in Lincoln. Or it simply could have been his love for them as believers with problems far too great for them to solve that drew his interest. Whatever the reason, she looked forward to his daily visits. He did not stay long, but there were always a few words of comfort and prayer. The first night Eugene was in the hospital, Pastor Lehman came and called her out into the hall.

"I just want you to know," he said, "that I am going to take the responsibility of getting blood donors for Eugene. Don't worry about it at all. I'll see that enough blood is given so that you won't have to buy any."

Later, as Ferne saw all those pints of blood going into Eugene's veins, she thanked God for the people who gave it. The donors were members of Pastor Lehman's church, and most of them were people the Clarks had never met. Yet they gave blood for him. Eugene and Ferne never could forget their kindness.

77

To her it was ironic that Dr. Reed decided on November 22 that they would have to risk an operation. That was Diane's birthday. Dr. Reed called Ferne into the hall outside Eugene's room to sign papers permitting the operation and absolving himself, the surgeon, and the hospital of responsibility in the event of Eugene's death. Without her signature the surgery would not be done.

"I wish I could tell you that the danger is no greater now than it was at the time of the first operation," he said to her. "But that would not be true, even though there was a high element of risk when surgery was performed in June. Given Gene's weakened condition, I have serious doubts about his coming through surgery, but we are caught in an extremely difficult position. Without the operation, we are positive that he will not live."

Ferne hesitated, praying for guidance. She did not know what to do. It sounded to her as though they were sure Eugene would die regardless of what they did. How could she sign to permit an operation that Dr. Reed did not believe Eugene had the strength to go through? How could she refuse to sign when not doing surgery meant certain death for Eugene?

She needed someone to advise her, to tell her what she should do. Yet there was no one to do that, no one who would take the awesome responsibility. This was a decision she had to make—alone. She looked up at Dr. Reed, who was waiting for her signature or word that she would not sign. He had already told her that he thought Eugene's only chance for living was in having surgery in a desperate effort to stop the bleeding. But he would not urge her. She had to make up her own mind about whether to sign the release.

She thought back to other times when Eugene and she had been facing difficult situations regarding his health. She had heard him say many times, as they prayed for healing, that he considered the skill and wisdom of doctors as much a part of divine healing as a miracle. Eugene had always trusted the judgment of this man who was with her. If she were the one who was lying in that hospital room, she knew what Eugene would do. Her hand was trembling so violently that she had difficulty holding the pen, but she signed her name. Then she cried.

Ferne supposes she phoned Mr. Epp or Mr. Jones or Pastor Lehman after that. She may have called all three. Those hours were a blur to her, like so much of that awful week. It was ten o'clock at night when they took Eugene into surgery. By that time the chapel at Bryan Memorial Hospital was filled with Broadcast co-workers and friends who had gathered spontaneously to pray for Eugene and Ferne.

She stood by his bed as they came in to take him. He had rallied a moment or two before, enough to know what was happening and that Ferne was there. His warm, assuring smile lighted his pain-distorted face, and he reached out and took her hand, squeezing it feebly. "See you soon, Kitty," he said softly, calling her by a pet name.

She stood in the long hall and watched as they wheeled him into surgery and closed the door. She did not move, although the darkened corridor was then empty. She was savoring that precious, fleeting instant when he had held her hand and spoken to her.

"I'm going to hang on to that," she told herself. "It's my promise that Eugene is going to live."

Someone had given them a copy of *Living Psalms and Proverbs* a short time before, and they had been reading from it. While she stood there a verse came to mind: "You have seen me tossing and turning through the night. You have collected all my tears and preserved them in your bottle! You have recorded every one in your book" (Psalm 56:8).

That was the verse for her. *God must have a lot of bottles up in heaven that have Ferne Clark's tears in them,* she thought. But Eugene had said that he would see her soon. That was evidence of his own assurance that he would come through the surgery.

Almost breathlessly she watched the door to the operating room. If it opened too soon, it would mean that it was all over and that Eugene was dead. Every minute that passed with the door closed was an encouragement. It meant that he had survived just that much more of the operation.

She does not remember praying so much that night as she does resting in His presence. It was as though His loving arms were around her, quieting her fears. She sensed that He was speaking to her troubled heart. She could not say that she had perfect peace. She was too distraught to allow God to have complete control, but she had a strength that had to have come from Him. There was no other explanation for the way she was able to stand up under the strain of those dreadful hours.

She could not help thinking about their three children. How would she be able to care for them alone? She was not thinking only about meeting their financial needs, as difficult as that would be. She was thinking about those other problems. How would she handle discipline as the boys got older? How would she counsel them and give them guidance? There were so many things that she instinctively expected Eugene to handle. If God took him, she would have to be responsible for them herself. And she did not see how she could do it.

An hour passed, then two hours. Still there was no movement of the door. Before the night was over, she knew well the power of the grace of God. She was in agony, yet she was at peace. She could not explain the churning mix of emotions within her that night, but she was sustained by a power far greater than her own.

Finally the operation was over and the door opened. She approached the surgeon, her mind full of apprehension. "How is he, doctor?" she asked, her voice breaking.

His gaze bore into hers, and then he smiled. "You will never believe it, Mrs. Clark," he said, "but your husband came through the surgery beautifully." He went on to tell her that there was a small geyser of blood when he made the incision. There was so much blood and clots of blood that they clogged the tubes they were using to remove it. "We took out all but about a fourth of his stomach," the surgeon continued. "It is good that we operated. He could never have lived without surgery."

She felt the strength drain from her knees, and tears of relief spilled from her eyes and ran down her cheeks. God had, indeed, guided her in signing for the operation. She went into Eugene's room and collapsed in a chair near his bed.

She sat there the rest of the night and the next day. He had lived through the operation, which was almost a miracle in itself, according to the surgeon, and it looked as though he was going to continue to improve, but she was drained emotionally. She had no strength, even to rejoice.

As the hours passed, it was obvious that Eugene was beginning to gain strength. His color improved and he was breathing easier. Still, she could not bring herself to leave his room. She remained in the chair as if in a trance.

That night when the head nurse* came in for a moment, Ferne had an opportunity to talk with her about the Lord. Although Ferne had witnessed con-

*She is the nurse who lived in the Clark neighborhood and who came over to the house in response to Ferne's call at the time of Eugene's first hemorrhage.

81

cerning Christ to her on several occasions, she was not a believer.† But she had been deeply concerned about both Eugene and Ferne.

The nurse talked about the shock of President Kennedy's assassination the previous afternoon. "You know, Ferne," she said impulsively, yesterday morning Jacqueline Kennedy had so much more than you have, but tonight you have so much more than she has."

Ferne had not thought about that before, but it was true. Money, or the lack of it, did not mean a thing in a situation like the one they found themselves in.

Once the hemorrhage had been stopped by surgery, Eugene began to improve quickly. In a few days he was sitting on the side of the bed, shaving. Nurses from all over the hospital would stop in to look at him. Word had been out that he was dying. Now he was on his way to recovery. He was such a miracle that they could scarcely believe it.

As he lay on the hospital bed after surgery, Eugene thought about the new arrangement "How Great Thou Art" that he had done for the Broadcast for its Thanksgiving banquet. He had known many occasions when God had revealed His greatness to him, but never one like the present time. How he wished he could get to an organ to make the hospital ring with His praises!

On Thanksgiving morning, Eugene was given a little food in the form of skimmed milk. He only took a taste, but it was ambrosia to him. The doctor came in a few minutes later.

"I think I just had the best meal I've ever eaten," Eugene told him.

The doctor smiled and took his wrist. "Son," he said quietly, "I guess we do have a lot to be thankful for, don't we?"

†She became a Christian some time later, after her own husband died.

82

8

Friends

Eugene was finally released from the hospital, and Ferne took him home. She had looked forward eagerly to that day ever since the doctor decided Eugene was well enough to be moved from intensive care. Yet she had a certain amount of apprehension. He was drawing sick benefits from his job, but they only amounted to half his earnings. They had so many doctor bills to meet, along with the normal expenses of living, that she was frightened. And she had the added responsibility of caring for him.

The problem was not that she did not want to care for him. She begrudged every moment she was not at his side. But there was so much to do—cleaning and cooking and taking care of the children—in addition to caring for him. Her concern came from a lack of confidence in her own ability to keep everything going and to make all the decisions until Eugene was strong enough to make them once more.

One of the most difficult things for her proved to be cooking during that period of adjustment. She found it hard to plan meals. Nothing sounded good to her. She does not know how the Berean ladies learned of her feelings about cooking those days. One of their number may have gone through a similar experience and remembered it. Whatever the reason, she was surprised when two of them appeared at the Clark door the afternoon Eugene got home and announced that they would like to bring them their meals three times a week. Ferne tried to protest, but they would not listen. "We *want* to help you," they said.

For weeks the women of the Berean Church brought them food to eat every other day. Ferne tried to thank them, but she could not fully express how much she appreciated their thoughtfulness. It was not only the help they gave that she appreciated; it was the knowledge that they cared, that they loved them and were praying for them.

It was the same with the people from the Broadcast. Women brought over food and stopped by to tell them that they were praying for them. Others were concerned about Ferne and volunteered to come in and stay with Eugene so that she could get away for a little while. It was a glorious experience that was just beginning—but they were not yet aware of that. They expected it to be over as soon as Eugene was on his feet and able to work again. Mercifully, God gave them one more Christmas before letting them understand what was ahead for them.

Eugene was released from the hospital a few days before the holiday. They set up their tree in the bedroom on the second floor, where he was in bed, and put all their gifts under it.

That was a wonderful Christmas. Years later it warmed Ferne's heart to think of it. The biggest present, of course, was that Eugene was home and the little family was together once more. They sang a few carols and quoted some Bible verses the kids had been learning, and Eugene told them the Christmas story again. The boys could have quoted it from memory themselves, but they liked to hear Daddy tell it.

84

Then they opened their packages. No one seemed to notice that the gifts were smaller than usual. They were all as happy and as excited as though theirs were the most expensive gifts ever given to anyone in Lincoln.

Before Eugene had left the hospital, the doctor had come in and sat on his bed to tell Ferne and him that he would no longer be able to prescribe cortisone for Eugene's arthritis. The side effects were too great. "I'm sure you're aware of the fact that cortisone has caused your ulcer and the two hemorrhages," he said.

Eugene nodded wordlessly. He was looking beyond the doctor at Ferne. A look of horror had filled her eyes. She knew as well as her husband how important the comparatively new drug had been in controlling his arthritis.

"What does that mean as far as the future is concerned?" he asked.

There was a long, pained silence. Ferne's cheeks were a pasty gray and her lower lip trembled. She was fighting hard to keep control of her frayed emotions.

"It's not the way I would like to have it," Dr. Reed began.

"And?" she managed to say.

He cleared his throat as though he were about to speak. Then, uncertain what to say, he got to his feet and stood at the window, looking out over the bleak, winter-lashed city. "Let's put it this way," he said gently. "Cortisone is the best medication for the control of arthritis available today. Unfortunately, it also has side effects that can be severe in some people. That happens to be the situation with you, Eugene."

"But what does that mean as far as his arthritis is concerned?" Ferne asked.

"We will have to wait and see," he told them.

When he spoke, Eugene thought he detected a hint of helplessness and frustration in his voice, but he could not be sure. "At the time of your first surgery after the first hemorrhage," the doctor continued, "I considered taking you off the drug. I knew what it had done to your stomach, and I was very much afraid you would not be able to survive a second surgery. Still, I was reluctant to take cortisone away from you because you need it so desperately."

Ferne had a few questions, which he answered as candidly as possible. It was then obvious that the conversation was over, but Dr. Reed seemed reluctant to leave that morning. He talked about other things with them, as though their secure little world was still standing strong and firm. A casual listener would have thought they had no problems more serious than those they were discussing. But that was because the full import of what he had said had not yet become real to them. The doctors had told them often that they should thank God for cortisone, that Eugene was totally dependent upon it, and that it was the only thing that was helping to keep his iritis in check. Yet, they did not fully understand the alternatives.

As soon as Dr. Reed left the room, Ferne ran to Eugene's bed and wrapped her arms around him in a trembling embrace. "It doesn't matter what he says, Eugene," she said. "God hasn't brought us this far to desert us now."

He nodded in agreement. However, he was thinking somewhat differently. She was clinging to the hope that God would not allow him to go blind. Eugene was assured that God would not forsake them, regardless of what came their way. He had fought that battle earlier—several years before when he lay in darkness and considered that the day might come when he would be permanently blind. He had fought against it and had cried out to the Lord until

He quieted his heart and brought him to the place of total submission. And there had been times during those first bewildering months of iritis when he wondered if God had deserted him; but by this time he had victory over his feelings of abandonment.

When he got home he spent most of his time in bed. But he forced himself to get up a few hours every day in an effort to regain his strength. They had a lot of visitors during the Christmas holidays and the cold and dismal month of January. It was good to see the friends who stopped to show their love and concern for them and to pray that Eugene's health would be restored.

Early in February, Eugene began to develop other problems. His stomach was so small that it would involuntarily contract whenever he ate, and he would faint. It frightened Ferne, although she tried to give him the impression that it did not bother her. Whenever it happened, she threw open the windows and fanned him until he regained consciousness. The frequency of the attacks increased until they were happening three times a day. His strength began to ebb again.

Even though Ferne tried to make herself believe that God was going to protect Eugene from the effects of iritis once he stopped taking cortisone, she really had no assurance that that would happen. She would wake up at night, sweat moistening her forehead and her body trembling. And in the morning a leaden iciness lay in the pit of her stomach. She trusted God. That was not the problem. Nor was she thinking about herself. She loved Eugene so very much that she could not stand to have anything else happen to him.

In mid-February, however, he had another serious attack, and the doctor thought he had hemorrhaged again. It happened one night after the children went to bed and were asleep. Ferne got a neighbor to stay with them, and she rushed him to the hospital, certain that he would not live until morning.

The incident had a terrifying effect on the children. It was the third time in less than a year that they went to bed, secure in the knowledge that their family was together, only to wake up in the morning and learn that Daddy was gone. Ferne tried to reassure them that Eugene would be all right, especially after they learned the cause of the trouble, but they had difficulty believing that this time was any different from the others. All three became nervous and irritable and had frequent crying spells. Grandpa and Grandma Clark, as best as they could, tried to help them understand, but it was difficult. In spite of everything any of them did, the children still would have bad dreams and wake up in the night, crying.

That stay in the hospital lasted five weeks, while the doctors tried a variety of bland diets in an effort to find foods Eugene could eat without going into shock. There was some improvement after a week or two, and Ferne was beginning to be encouraged.

Then she noticed his hands. They were all right when he went to the hospital, and she did not notice how long it was after he got there that they were first affected by arthritis. Still, she remembers very distinctly everything that happened the morning she first noticed them. She walked cheerily into his room, sat on the side of the bed, and kissed him.

"How is it going today, Gene?" she asked.

"Fine. Fine," he said. That was a stock answer for him. It did not make any difference how bad he felt; he always said he was fine.

She told him about the children and that Diane was drawing him another belated valentine, complete with hearts and kisses and a snowman. Then she happened to glance at his hands. At first she noticed nothing unusual about them. She had been with him every day, and the daily changes were so subtle that she had difficulty recognizing them. So it was with his hands. On that morning she looked away and then realized that they were not normal. Her gaze whipped back, and for the first time she understood that they were different from before. The joints were swollen, and it seemed that his fingers had stiffened. Always before they had been quick and supple. Now she saw that he could use them only with conscious effort.

A dreadful chill swept over her. *Dear God! Not his hands! He'll die if he can't play the piano and the organ! Not his hands!*

But they were affected. There was no doubt of that. "Have you been having problems with your hands?" she finally managed to ask.

"Yes."

She wanted to cry, but she could not. The hurt was too deep for tears. "How long have you noticed it?"

His eyes were tender and compassionate—filled with concern for her, even though he was the one who might never be able to play his beloved instrument again. "I first began to notice it several days ago," he said. Then, feeling guilty because he had kept it from her, he explained. "You've had so much lately, I just couldn't tell you about it yet. I decided it was best not to let you know until you saw it for yourself."

That day they both faced up to the fact that, without cortisone to keep it in check, his arthritis was like a forest fire out of control. It roared through his body like one berserk, robbing muscles and joints of mobility and exacting a terrible toll in pain. His thumbs eventually pulled back until they touched his wrists and could no longer be controlled. And his neck! That ugly, invisible force pulled his head to the left until his ear all but touched the bone, and held it there. The muscles in

89

his neck were taut and immobilized, and the veins and cords stood out like ropes. Those were days of horror and dread as the changes took place. They were worse for his distraught wife than for the children, but difficult enough for all the family. And there was nothing anyone could do to help him.

Ferne could think of little else from the time she woke up in the morning until she went to bed at night. She tried to avoid looking at his hands and the way his head was drawn to one side, but she could not. Every time she went into his room her gaze was drawn to them, like iron to a magnet. She would stare in growing agony at his long fingers, as though she were actually seeing his arthritis worsen, hour by hour.

There were times during those difficult days when Eugene thought that he had reached the end of his endurance. *Lord!* he cried out, *I can't go any farther. This is it!* And on one occasion he complained to Ferne, "Is there anything else that could happen to us? Hasn't it all happened?"

For a time after the arthritis began to rob him of his hands, he felt as though their world had collapsed on them. But there was more to come. There were times when he was so crushed by the weight of his affliction that he would turn on his side in bed and say, *"Lord, I don't know why I can't take any more. I don't want to be this way, but I can't take another day of this pain and uncertainty and trouble. You have to put it together for me again.*

He was not telling God that He had to heal him because of the terrible load the family had been carrying. He was willing to accept the burden if God would help him. He was reminding Him that he had reached the limit of his endurance.

At other times he could not even pray. There was no sense in being hypocritical about it. He was so overwhelmed by circumstances and was feeling so sorry for himself at those times that he was not capable of praying right then.

Things were even worse when he lost the use of his fingers. He had been practicing the piano and organ for thirty years. There had been long, lonely hours spent to gain proficiency. He had worked other long, lonely hours mastering skills in arranging and composing. And he had a position of importance in music at the Broadcast. His hands had become his life.

He did not realize that his fingers were so badly deformed until his thumb touched something it shouldn't have.The first time it happened he ignored it, as though that would make the problem disappear. The next time, he *knew* what had happened and was stunned by it. The realization that his hands were crooked slammed into his consciousness like a wrecker's ball turning a brick building into rubble. He could accept his going blind. He could accept the crippling of his body, as difficult as that would be. But his hands!

Dear Lord! he cried out in agony. *Not my hands. Not my hands!*

But there was no denying what had happened to them. Arthritis had twisted them ruthlessly. He realized, even before he was willing to accept the fact, that he would never be able to play again. It did not matter whether he would be able to see or get up and walk around. The music within his heart was locked there, and God seemingly had thrown away the key.

Later God was going to make it possible for him to continue with an important part of his ministry, but He was not ready then to reveal that to him. Days had to pass while Eugene wrestled with his burden. Then he would see His deliverance.

During the years he had had arthritis, iritis, and glaucoma, Eugene had learned much about them.

He could recognize the most minute symptoms that indicated a new attack or the lessening of one. He knew when a different joint was affected and the instant the pain began to increase. So he was very much aware of the change being wrought in his fingers and hands.

He knew his arthritis was worse than it had ever been and that it was an affliction that would not stop. He felt it in his wrists and elbows and knees and in an irresistible drawing of his head to one side. He tried to make himself believe that the therapy and hot packs were helping and that the attack would soon ease. The new treatment had made a little difference. He seemed to get better just before he was released from the hospital. Yet, deep within, he knew that any gain, barring a miracle, was only temporary. Medically speaking, he would never be able to play the organ or piano again.

He was sure that no one—not even Ferne—knew the depth of his hurt as he realized the fearsome cost the arthritis was exacting. Music—after God, Ferne, and his family—was the most important thing in his life. He was happiest when he was composing or arranging or pouring out his love for God in a torrent of melodious sound.

Now, as far as he could determine, that part of his life was over; at least the playing part was finished. And he did not know whether he would be able to continue carrying out his other responsibilities in the music department of the Broadcast, or if they would even want him. Music was so important in the production of the daily programs that they might think they needed someone unhandicapped by illness.

He was also concerned about caring for his family. He could not expect the Broadcast to keep him on the payroll. They had a responsibility to their donors to use wisely and frugally the money that came in. No one at the Broadcast mentioned the prospect of discontinuing the check he received every pay period, but he thought a lot about it, wondering when it would stop.

Eugene and Ferne prayed often about their needs, asking God to help them financially and to help them trust Him for their care. Trusting God was one of those things that was easy to talk about, but to actually do it was something else. It was not easy to trust God to provide and not to worry or be concerned when they saw their meager supply of dollars dwindling, with no decrease in demand. In the weeks that followed they learned to trust God completely for their care, but it did not come easily. More often than not, Ferne and Eugene tried to peer into their bleak future, faltering, as they spent night after night awake, trying to figure out how they could manage.

Always they reached the same conclusion. There was no way they could take care of their obligations and meet the financial demands of a family. Yet, they had to. Despite their fears and lack of faith, they had to trust God. There was no one else to help them.

Ferne loved their house and had loved it ever since the real estate agent first showed it to them a number of years before. Yet, for some strange reason there was a subtle change in her attitude toward it after Eugene's second hemorrhage. She began to dislike those familiar rooms, because there was so much in them to remind her of the bad things that had happened to them. She wanted to go as far away from that house as possible. She tried to push those thoughts aside, feeling a little foolish for harboring them. At least that was what she did until Eugene was taken to the hospital following a blackout. Then all her hostilities and frustrations

93

centered on the house, as though it were to blame for his illness.

She will never forget the day she went into his room in the hospital and informed him that she was going to see a real estate agent the next morning and list their house for sale.

He gasped and tried to sit up in bed. "What did you say, Ferne?" he asked.

"I'm going to list our house for sale," she announced with the finality of one who has made up her mind and is determined not to be reasoned with.

"But why?" he asked, bewildered. "I thought you liked it."

"I do." By this time she was close to tears, but she was determined not to cry. If she did she would not be able to finish what she had to tell him. She did not know how, but she had to get it across to him that she meant what she said. "But I—I—I can't go back to that place," she blurted. "It has too many bad memories."

He was staring incredulously at her, as though she was suddenly bereft of her senses. "Oh," he said quite calmly for someone who had had a bomb like that dropped on him. "Really?"

"It may sound silly to you," she continued, on the edge of hysteria, "but I just can't go home there any more. I feel as though I can't spend another night in that house unless I know for sure that we are going to get rid of it."

Eugene did not laugh at her. She was so overwrought that she would have exploded into anger if he had. Of course, it was not his way to laugh at people. Patiently and lovingly he talked with her. He went over their financial condition in some detail, explaining that they could not increase their obligations at such a time. He knew being in the house where so much had happened was hard for her, but they did not even know whether he would be able to work again, or how soon he could go back if he would be able to work. They could not seriously consider getting another house right then.

As he talked, her heart began to quiet, and a new warmth and peace came over her. It was not the things he said. She knew, even before she sprang her surprise decision upon him, that it was unwise. Her help came from the assurance that Eugene knew about her problem and understood how she felt. He honestly cared, even though she was being unreasonable in her demands. When she left the hospital two or three hours later, she was calm and content to return home. She found, to her amazement, that her revulsion against the house had vanished. She began to love each familiar board even more than before. It was again "home" to her, but in an even more wonderful way than it had previously been.

When Eugene was released from the hospital, they rented a hospital bed, which they set up in the dining room. He had to spend a great deal of his time in it. He was able at first to get out to the car at regular intervals to go to the hospital for therapy. But it was not long before even so brief a trip was too much for him. He had a great deal of difficulty walking out to the car and into the hospital. When Tom Journey, the therapist, learned of his predicament, he came out to the house on his own time to continue the treatments. He was determined that they were going to overcome the effects of his arthritis, and he did everything he could think of to help Eugene.

Eugene seemed to realize that he was losing a little ground every week—not much, but enough so that he was aware of it. He steadily had a little less strength in his legs and arms, his fingers and knees became stiffer and less movable and his eyesight was gradually deteriorating. He did not say

95

anything to Tom about it, however. The therapist was so determined to get him going again that Eugene did not want to hurt him. Eugene was sure, however, that Tom knew, although Tom did not mention it, either. He was a dedicated, perceptive young man, more skilled than most in his field. He came to the house week after week for months before accepting defeat.

Eugene will never forget the night when he and Tom decided that he had to try to walk again. Actually, Tom was the one who suggested that he try. Eugene did not know whether he had planned it for that night or decided suddenly. Tom looked at Ferne and then at Eugene. "How about it?" he asked. "Shall we go from the bed to the front room?"

He sounded so sure that Eugene could make it that Eugene took heart from the therapist's confidence. "Why not?" he said.

Tom and Ferne helped him sit up in bed and stand. His legs were rubbery and he almost collapsed on their shoulders.

"You OK?" Tom asked quickly.

"I'm all right now. I've got my balance."

"If you're ready, let's go."

He tried, but it was no use. His legs folded under him every time he tried to move. After a painful two or three minutes Eugene said, "I'm sorry, Tom. It's no go. My legs just won't work."

No one mentioned it, but as he got into bed, all three were aware that he would never leave it under his own power unless God gave him new strength and arthritis-free joints.

Eugene L. Clark

Eugene Clark (on the right, at age 12) with bicycle he earned from his parents for learning to play his first 25 hymns. —see story

Eugene Clark, (age 16) playing the piano in the family living room where he prayed to receive Christ after playing an invitational hymn and wrote his first composition.

Eugene Clark at the piano, senior recital time—Moody Bible Institute.

Eugene Clark at the organ.

Eugene and Ferne Clark on their engagement day.

*Eugene and Ferne coming down the aisle
after the wedding.*

Back to the Bible studio picture while Eugene (seated at the organ) was organist-producer.

Clark family portrait just before Eugene became bedfast. (1962)

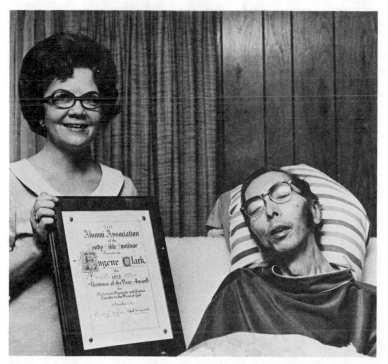

Eugene and Ferne Clark holding his 1973 Moody Alumnus of the year award.

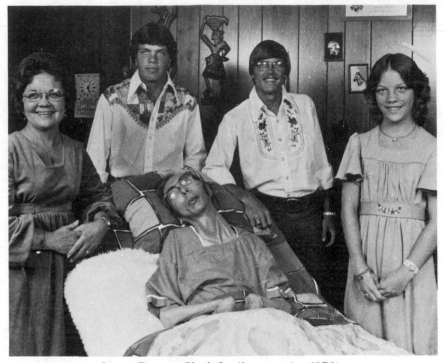

Latest Eugene Clark family portrait. (1976)

Ferne *Bryan* *Bruce* *Diane*

Eugene

9

"A Friend Loveth
at All Times"

Eugene was not going to walk again. That became abundantly plain to Ferne after Tom Journey tried to help him negotiate the brief distance from his bed, which had been set up in the dining room, to the living room. Eugene could still stand by bracing himself, but his frail legs lacked mobility, and Ferne could see that he was getting progressively weaker.

It was even more difficult for her to acknowledge that a form of the same illness that chained his body was also stealing his sight. Without cortisone the iritis attacks were more frequent and savage in intensity. And every bout with the dread disease touched another match to his glaucoma, burning out a bit more of his ability to see.

It was not long before he could distinguish only light from dark, and the medication he was still allowed to take had little effect on his wasted body. Both Eugene and Ferne knew that their worst fears were being realized. He was crippled so badly with arthritis that he was permanently bedridden, and he would soon be completely blind.

They talked at length with their children about it. They had never kept anything from them since they were old enough to understand, and they were not going to begin in this situation. They wanted them to know the exact nature of Eugene's physical problems and what they could expect in the future. He insisted on that.

Ferne made his room the center of their family activity. The family had been separated for such a long time while he was in the hospital. There was a danger of the children's getting used to managing without him and continuing to live their lives with him on the fringe; he would be looking on but never a part of them. She was determined that that was not going to happen, so they had his bed placed in the dining room on the main floor. It meant rearranging much of the house, but he was close to the kitchen and the living room, where the children and Ferne spent so much time.

At first Eugene protested that it meant too much disruption for them, but Ferne would not listen to him. "No way," she protested firmly. "If you're upstairs you'll be out of what's going on, most of the time. You won't get to meet the kids' friends when they come over, and besides, you're the head of the house. I want you down here where you can help me with discipline and the other decisions that have to be made."

She meant it. She was tired of being both father and mother to their children. She was tired of having to depend on her own judgment when she was so uncertain about so many things and Eugene was able to help her. He knew how to handle the boys, and Diane was his devoted slave. If she even suspected that he was displeased about something she had done, she was inconsolable until he had taken her up on his bed and kissed away her tears.

Then there was the matter of finances. Ferne had, of necessity, been brought up to be frugal. She knew how to shop for bargains and plan economical menus. She could get the most out of a limited clothes budget and keep their light, heat, and water bills to a minimum. It was the big decisions she had to wrestle with that bothered her so much. What did she do about house payments and taxes and a leak in the roof? When was it wise to make repairs, and when should they replace an item?

And then there was the car. All she knew about motors was that they used gas and oil and sometimes developed asthma or the flu or some other strange, internal disease that completely baffled her. Their cars always seemed to have something wrong with them in those days. She did not know what to have repaired and what to let go. Eugene would often ignore a noisy symptom for months, knowing it would not develop into anything serious. The next time he would take the car to the garage at the first hint of some new ailment that did not concern her at all. She really needed Eugene's judgment and help. And she supposed it was best for him that she did.

As soon as he was feeling well enough, he had her get in touch with the savings and loan company that held the mortgage on their house. He had taken out a special insurance policy that would make their house payments for five years in case he was not able to work. That removed one immediate problem. They were not going to lose their home, at least for that length of time. Still, they had some adjustments to make. They did not know what they were going to do for money to live on. Eugene was still drawing money from the Broadcast, but they knew that could not continue indefinitely. The company would not be able to keep him on the payroll for long.

Ferne's going to work was out of the question. She had a home to keep up and an invalid husband and three lively children to care for. She was desperately needed at home. But that was not the only reason they refused to consider her working. Neither Eugene nor Ferne have any quarrel with wives who work outside the home. Each situation is different, and each couple has to decide what is best for them; but they had reached a conclusion on the matter even before they were married. As long as they were childless, Ferne would work if they thought it necessary; but when they had children, she was going to stay home and take care of them.

They realized all of that, but it was difficult for Ferne to be objective when it seemed that their needs were so great and their resources so small. They prayed—how they prayed! But there was no break in the heavy, churning clouds of bewilderment and doubt.

She was to discover, however, that God was even more concerned about their welfare than they were themselves and that He was beginning to move. But He was not ready to reveal His plans for their lives just yet. Ferne had not learned enough about trusting Him. He wanted to teach her that He was their answer for every situation.

God had been dealing with Ferne for years. She has always thought that He began to work in her life when she was a child and her mother, older sister, and she had had such a difficult time financially. And He had continued to mold her through the years as Eugene's health grew progressively worse. Then, with him blind and confined to his bed with a crippling form of arthritis, she realized that their problems could not be solved by their own ingenuity. She had to look to Him.

God knew Ferne well enough to know that He had to crush her pride and an almost stupid determination to work everything out on her own. So she thought and planned and schemed and accomplished nothing. And she and Eugene prayed, but for a time there was no answer. It was as though the ears of God were stopped or He was suddenly beyond hearing them. Finally, when they were at the place of complete helplessness—when they could see that He and He alone could meet their needs and that their total trust had to be in Him— He began to move.

People stopped by regularly to see Eugene. In itself, that was not unusual. It had been happening for years, whenever he was ill. But men and women started coming whom they scarcely knew, stopping to visit for a few minutes and to pray with them. Often they brought a few cans of vegetables or some meat or potatoes.

They do not know how Eugene came up with the idea of dictating his music and having someone transcribe it for him. Of course he had dictated his letters when he was at the office. That may have given him the idea. And, of course, he was praying a great deal about being able to do something to support Ferne and the children. Once he got the idea and thought about it enough to be convinced that it was practical, he had to sell the plan to the people at the Broadcast.

They were not sure he could do it, and various reasons for not trying were advanced. It would take another musician, for one thing, and each musician has his own style. They could envision all sorts of problems—personality clashes as the two tried to work together, a disruption of work in the department, and difficulty in getting anything done.

But Eugene was sure his plan would work. "I'm sure I can do it," he said, "whether anyone else thinks I can or not."

Ferne agreed with him. Even though she did not really know that much about arranging and writing music, she had complete confidence in her husband.

101

She knew that his music was not in his twisted, arthritic fingers. It was in his heart. Neither a crippling arthritis nor blindness could keep him from music. All he had to do was figure how to get the notes on paper, and he would be able to arrange and compose as well as he had when he had been able to see and play.

As Eugene lay in bed, he gave a great deal of thought to how he could do arranging and composing. He was not physically able to try it yet, but as soon as he felt strong enough he wanted to get to work. The very thought that he might still be able to serve God by continuing some of his responsibilities at the Broadcast was exhilarating.

He contacted the Department of the Visually Impaired and Handicapped of the state of Nebraska and was able to secure dictating equipment. Although he did not feel up to working yet, he tried the machine enough to know that he would be able to arrange and compose with it. The day he made that discovery he was excited and happy. It had been a long while since he had known such joy. The knowledge that he would again be able to write music and support his family was an encouragement he could not express. He was no longer helpless. It was true that he was confined to his bed and racked with arthritis. It was also true that he would never see again. But, praise God, he was not helpless. It was not going to be easy, but he did not have to turn the responsibility of caring for Ferne and their children over to others. He could still function as the head of the house. How he thanked God for that. He felt a new joy and strength surging through him that set his heart to singing.

During the weeks and months after Eugene was released from the hospital, Eugene and Ferne continually saw evidences of Christian love that brought tears to their eyes and prayers of praise and thanksgiving to their lips. There were so many who went so far out of their way to help them.

When he first came home from the hospital, Eugene still required almost constant care. Ferne slept on a couch in the living room, and Eugene would whistle when he needed her. The children were sleeping upstairs, but they figured that if one of them needed her, they could run down and get her or yell loud enough to wake her. Eugene had to call her to help him turn in bed, to get his medication, or to help him with the bedpan or the urinal. She did not know what it was to sleep through an entire night without interruption. And in addition to looking after him, she had to spend hours with him every day in therapy. The hours were not numerous enough or long enough to permit her to get everything done. And she had the kids to look after as well.

It was during this period that Diane caught a cold that worsened and turned into the croup. She was getting blue and fighting for breath when the doctor arrived. "You've got to get her to the hospital right away," he said.

She was in the hospital for a week. During that time the Berean and Broadcast ladies took over.* They fixed the family's meals and worked out a schedule so that someone was at the house all the time that she was away at the hospital.

It was during that period that Ferne got well acquainted with Virginia Ashcraft. Virginia lived in their neighborhood, and they were casually acquainted before Diane became ill. When Virginia heard about the latest illness in the family, she told

---

*Only God, who keeps the record, could possibly know the names of all those who have helped the Clarks over the years. To them, Eugene and Ferne give a special "Thank you," even though they may be unnamed in these pages.

a mutual friend that she was going over to the Clark home. "That woman needs help," she said.

She came over, and she and Ferne sat in the kitchen, drinking coffee, while she explained the purpose of her visit. "So," she concluded, "if you will let me, I'll come one day a week and help you."

If she would let her? She was sent from God! Eugene had to be turned every thirty minutes, day and night, along with the other care. Ferne begrudged him none of it, but there was a limit to what one person could do, especially without proper rest. And right then Ferne felt as though she could not keep going.

She thought, at first, that she would have to be with Virginia all the time she was working, telling her what to do and where things were. But Virginia proved to be one of those efficient individuals who instinctively knows what needs doing. Ferne told her where things were and dropped, exhausted, into a chair to rest. Virginia went about the job as efficiently as if she were in her own home, and when Ferne tried to thank her later, Virginia seemed embarrassed.

"It's little enough to do for you," she said. "I'm glad I can help." At the front door she told Ferne that she would be back again the following week. She did not ask if Ferne wanted her to come or give her opportunity to refuse. She saw that Ferne needed help, and she was going to see that she got it. It was as simple as that.

Crying out of gratitude, Ferne went in to tell Eugene what had happened. She was sure that, being a man, he did not understand how she felt. He could not have known how frustrating it had been for her to see the housework pile up; never to get finished with the cleaning. She knew that those visitors who came to see Eugene would understand when the papers and clothes were not picked up and there was dust on the furniture. Yet, she was humiliated when she saw that the house was not as clean as it should have been.

Now she need not worry about that. Virginia Ashcraft was taking care of that for her. Her friend did not stop helping when the immediate crisis was over, either. She continued to come and clean for Ferne for nine years. When she was offered a job she accepted on one condition, that she be given Thursdays off so that she could go over to the Clarks' house and help.

A few years later, when Ferne became ill suddenly with a bowel obstruction, she staggered to the phone at four in the morning and called Virginia, telling her what was happening. Virginia was over at the house almost as soon as Ferne hung up the phone. And when Virginia finally gave up her self-appointed task of cleaning for Ferne, it was because an arthritic condition in her elbows made it impossible for her to do such work. She even had to stop doing her own cleaning.

Eugene looked after fixing things around the house as long as he was able, but the time came when that was impossible. That troubled him greatly. Ferne had enough to do taking care of the children and the house and him, and they could not afford to hire someone. It was then that Jack Ashcraft, Virginia's husband and the man in charge of maintenance at the Broadcast, must have sensed his concern. He came over one evening and announced that he was going to keep up the place for them. He lived only a block away, so it was easy for him to stop in from time to time and check to see that everything was in order. "But don't wait for me to come," he said. "If you've got any problems with the plumbing or have a light switch that needs fixing, give me a call." And when he heard that they would like to panel their basement, he came over and did the work.

When Eugene was released from the hospital in February 1964, he would not allow Ferne or anyone else to talk about buying a hospital bed. "We'll rent," he announced firmly. "There's no use in buying an expensive item like that and have it in the way when I'm up and around again." He was determined not to stay on his back, even though he knew the doctor's opinion.

But as the months wore on, it became apparent that he was going to need a hospital bed much longer than he would admit. And there were other problems. After he had lain in one position for thirty or forty minutes, his body would ache so much that he would have to be moved. During the daytime that was not so bad, but at night he had to wake up Ferne. He did not want to wake her, and at first he tried to endure the pain through the night, but that was not possible. If he lay in one position more than half an hour, the pain was excruciating.

Eugene did not know how Jim Russel heard about his need to be turned throughout the night, but Jim and his wife, Evelyn, both worked at the Broadcast and were regular in visiting the Clarks. Eugene supposed they had been at the house when Ferne helped him change position, and perhaps Jim questioned them about it. In any event, Jim said one evening, "If you'll let me, I'll come over once a week and sleep on the couch so Ferne can get a full night's rest."

Eugene hesitated before replying. It was not that he was unappreciative or unmindful that Ferne needed a good night's rest at least once a week. But Eugene had been helped to turn by people who did not know how to turn him, and he had found the pain agonizing.

Jim seemed to sense his concern. "My dad was an arthritic and was confined to his bed," he explained.

"I used to take care of him all the time, so I know how to handle a person in your condition." Eugene soon learned that Jim was as gentle and tender as Ferne and his parents in helping him change positions. He could relax completely when Jim was there to put his arms around him and help him move. He knew exactly what to do to avoid hurting him.

From then on, Jim Russel was there at least once a week to stay with Eugene. He joined the older Mr. and Mrs. Clark in taking turns at the house so that Ferne could get away for a little while. This was especially true after she began getting requests to speak throughout Nebraska and the surrounding states. Jim and Evelyn were like part of the family, and the time came when they sold their home in another part of Lincoln and bought one in the immediate neighborhood of Eugene and Ferne so that they would be more readily available.

After Eugene had been bedfast for a few years, Wendell Tallaksen, chief radio engineer at the Broadcast, realized Eugene's need for a power-operated bed. At that time Eugene had one of the old variety with cranks, and every time his bones began to ache from being in one position too long and he wanted to move to ease the pain, Ferne or whoever was staying at the house had to come in and help him. He and Ferne knew how much easier an electric bed would be for both of them, but they did not have the money to buy one. Then Wendell saw the need.

"I'll put up the first hundred dollars to buy Gene a bed," he told some of the people at work. It was not long before enough came in to buy one. Wendell even changed the controls so that Eugene could operate them by himself with his crippled hands.

Help seemed to be volunteered exactly at the time they needed it most. Ferne tried to be as well organized as possible, but occasionally she would get bogged down and frustrated. The work around the house would pile up as the demands on her time increased, and she would get depressed by her own ineffectiveness. Almost invariably when that happened, someone would appear, quite unexpectedly, to take over.

That was the situation when Mrs. Theodore Epp stopped by on one of her periodic visits. "Mrs. Clark," she said quietly, "I know what it is to have more work to do than there are hours in the day. May I come over and help you? I can scrub and wax floors or do the washing or ironing or anything else that you need help with."

But there were also visitors of a different kind. They were just as concerned about the family, Eugene said, although there were times when Ferne found that difficult to believe. Some came in love, sincerely wanting to help. Others had the self-righteous accusations expressed by Job's friends.

Both Eugene and Ferne believed that God could heal and had earnestly sought God's leading. Some people sent them books from "faith healers" and urged them to attend their meetings. Even though they both knew that God has the power to heal and were looking for Him to do what the medical profession could not do, they could not believe that going to such a public service was within the will of the Lord for them. They redoubled their prayers that God would intercede.

Ferne was particularly strong in her conviction that Eugene's sight was going to be miraculously restored and that he would regain complete use of those marvelous, talented hands that had been dedicated to the service of the Lord. She had often lain in bed and thought about the wonder and joy of that moment when Eugene would first see again and be able to take her in his arms. She thought of the excitement he would know just by looking at Diane and Bruce and Bryan. They were so small when his sight blurred and faded. Now they were growing and changing every day. And to hear him play the organ or piano once more would be a joy that would almost equal hearing a heavenly chorus. That would be an occasion! She got so excited just thinking about it that she felt as though it could happen at any moment. *Lord,* she would pray, *let it happen right now. Tonight! Let Eugene call out to me to come in, telling me that You have restored his body.*

But it did not happen. Month after month after month they prayed and, although God answered many other prayers for them, it was as though His ears were closed against their pleas for healing.

That did not stop the devotees of divine healing from writing to Eugene or coming to see him, however. Eugene got letters from all over the country, telling him that it was not God's will that any should miss the blessing of healing and that unconfessed sin was all that stood between him and a miracle. It was difficult for Ferne to read the letters, but it was even more difficult for her to be nice to such people when they came to the house. They were so sure that they were right, so dogmatic in labeling Eugene a sinner of the grossest kind.

A few of the devotees were people Eugene and Ferne knew. Some of those were from Lincoln, and others drove in from a distance, thinking that God had directed them to show Eugene what he had to do to be healed. Ferne was soon usually able to recognize the purpose of their visit when she answered their knock. It was not that they looked or dressed differently from anyone else. It may have been the look in their eyes or the set to their jaws, as though they had to steel themselves against a possible outburst from either Eugene or Ferne. Ferne had to admit to being human enough to feel like turning them away, but Eugene did not want that. So she invited them in and stood by, seething inwardly, while they castigated him.

"It is because of sin in your life," some would tell him. "The Lord has revealed to me that it is because of pride that you haven't been healed. You've grown proud of your position with Back to the Bible and of all the publicity you've been given. If you want to be healed you will have to resign your position and humble yourself. Then God will work a miracle in your body."

Dear God, Ferne prayed silently in anguish. *How can they say such things about Eugene? You know that there is no gross pride in him. You know that he has never sought publicity and only wants to serve You! They don't know him. How can they talk the way they do? How can they be so certain that sin is the thing that is keeping Eugene like he is?*

Those visitors had Scripture to "prove" their position. Some used one set of verses; some another; and a third group would find something else; but the conclusions were the same. Eugene was not being healed because of arrogance and pride.

Ferne could not understand how Eugene could be so calm and kind. She was seething at their arrogance and unfairness in judging her husband without knowing him. But he was even-tempered and unruffled despite the accusations made against him. He explained that if he was proud, he was sorry. His main purpose in life was to serve his Lord in the way he had been called to serve Him. If God directed him to leave the Broadcast, he would not hesitate to do so, but he had to be sure of the Lord's leading.

"Why don't you tell them that your relationship with the Lord is between you and God?" Ferne would demand hotly after such an encounter. "They have no right to stand there and tell you that you're sinning when they know nothing about you."

"Now, Ferne," he would say quietly. "They mean well. Besides, we have to be very careful in our dealings with fellow believers. It could just be that God might be using them to chastise us."

She was furious and had to ask God to forgive her and to give her a forgiving spirit toward those people. She could much more easily have taken criticism of her own attitudes and actions. She knew how far short she fell of being what she should be. But Eugene! Such talk was ridiculous and so unfair that she wanted to lash out at the accusers.

They had gone a month or more without such a visitor when there was a knock on the door one cold, wintry afternoon. Ferne let a stranger into their living room. She was a thin, waspish little woman, hawk-faced and bent slightly at the shoulders. She carried a huge purse that must have been bulging with books. "I've come to see Mr. Clark," she announced sternly.

Ferne hesitated. Eugene had not been feeling too well for the past few days, and the signs indicated that this caller was of much the same sort as so many of the others.

"He's here, isn't he?" the woman demanded.

Ferne does not know why the woman asked the question. She could see him from where she stood. Ferne ushered her into the dining room that had been converted into a hospital room and waited. The elderly woman stopped at the foot of the bed, her frail fingers working nervously with the top of the bag.

"God has revealed your sin to me," she began. At first her voice quavered, but as she spoke she seemed to gain strength. "He has refused to heal your body because of the way you have sinned against music composers."

111

Eugene gasped and Ferne stared incredulously at her. They both had some difficulty believing that they had heard her correctly. "What do you mean?" he asked.

"You don't allow the Broadcast to play the music the way the composer wanted it to sound," she said. "You work it over until it's something entirely different."

"But that isn't the way it is," he tried to tell her. "Everybody does arranging. It's a very important part of music."

"It isn't Christian."

"If a male quartet wants to sing a number the composer has written for a soprano soloist," he tried to explain, "it has to be written in a different key or male voices would be unable to sing it."

"That is only an excuse," she persisted.

"But I arrange my own music."

"It is a sin against the composer and against God for anyone to tamper with a musical composition." Her voice raised. "That is the reason you are lying there blind and helpless. God is punishing you for what you are doing. If you will confess your sin and stop doing this dastardly thing, He will restore your health."

Ferne does not remember what Eugene said to her, except that he was gentle and considerate. He explained his own convictions on the subject and listened until she ended her tirade against him. The quiet way in which he talked to her made Ferne even more proud of him. In all the times that people came through the years, not once did Ferne hear him lose his temper, regardless of the charges they made against him.

10

"Take a Song"

As soon as Eugene had the strength, he went back to work, arranging music for the Broadcast choir, the quartet, and other singing groups. It was difficult to figure out exactly how to go about it, in spite of his training and years of experience. He could see neither the music nor the arrangement he was working on. And, even though he might have known the number from memory, he could not play it through.

But God had placed a piano in his heart. He could not actually hear the playing of that majestic instrument, nor did he have the power to make himself believe he was hearing a familiar number. It was a more subtle thing, brought into being, in part at least, by a loving God. His training and years of practice had something to do with it, of course, but it had to be more than that. As he recalled a hymn or an aria, it was as though he could see the music staff before him, complete with all the notes and special markings. He could feel the melody and the full-bodied harmony that added power and strength. More important for him now, he could visualize the composition as he had memorized it and play with the tune in his mind. He could work out pleasing little variations that would

113

add spark to an old, familiar hymn, as well as the mechanical work necessary to rewrite the number so that it could be sung by a male quartet, a ladies' trio, a mixed sextet, or whatever other group the music director had in mind.

There were still problems to be worked out, even though Eugene was able to dictate his music. He had to have the copy transcribed, returned to him at the house, and then played so that he could correct the mistakes before the final draft was made. The success or failure of his plan depended on finding someone who had the ability to transcribe the material.

And his plan meant a considerable sacrifice on the part of the one who worked with him. It had to be someone who was knowledgeable in music and, as the people in authority at the Broadcast pointed out, such individuals were accustomed to doing their own arranging. Working with Eugene meant that this person would have to push his own ideas and desires aside temporarily and write what Eugene wanted in the way he wanted it. He could well understand how difficult that would be. Yet, through the years God provided this expert assistance for him in the persons of Karolyn Wiebe, Jack Schrader, John Bertsch, and David Clydesdale. Without them, Eugene would have been unable to continue as he had planned.

He remembers well the first hymn he wrote after going blind and being confined to his bed. He worked out the lyrics, going over them in his mind again and again until he had them exactly the way he wanted them. Then he asked Ferne to write down the poem.

His heart was singing so joyously at being able to work again that it was not surprising that he wrote a new hymn in a few weeks, as soon as they had their procedures developed and functioning smooth-

114

ly. He did the lyrics first. Then he had Ferne record them in a spiral notebook that they kept for that purpose.

Once the rough draft was on paper, he was not afraid of losing the poem, and he began to go over it with Ferne. They worked on the lyrics, line by line and word by word, until they were completely satisfied that they had a pleasing poem that said what he wanted it to say. When they reached that point, they punctuated it and he spoke it into a dictation machine exactly as they wanted it typed. The typing was done in the office, and the copy came back to them. Then he was ready to go to work.

By that time a melody had begun to form in his mind. He hummed the tune on tape, but that would not have been necessary. It was scribed into his very being. Composing had always been enjoyable, but writing this song meant even more to him than the others. He had begun to doubt whether he would ever be able to write another piece of music. Now he knew that he would.

"Take a song!" he said. "This is a hymn setting for the poem called 'God Cannot Make a Mistake.' We will work on just two staffs. Basically this is a four-part hymn. I will give you the soprano, alto, tenor, and bass chord by chord. We will work in the key of B flat. It's in 6/4 rhythm. The first chord is: a quarter note chord with the base on B. Second line, the tenor on B above the staff. The alto is on D, a step above middle C, and soprano is on F, first space."

The next time Karolyn Wiebe, the girl from the Broadcast who was working with him, came to the house, she took the dictation belt back with her and transcribed the new song. Then she brought back the rough copy and played it for him on the piano so that he could hear it. She had recorded the hymn at

115

the same time so that he could play it again if he needed to.

Working alone at the house, Eugene made a few changes in the melody and worked out the harmony. After correcting that copy, Karolyn made a final draft, which they again checked for sound. Once the music was the way he wanted it, she typed in the words so that it could be put in a songbook or duplicated for the choir.

When he was writing a new hymn, the children always heard it a lot around the house, because he had to play it over and over to make corrections. "This one's going to be a hit," Ferne told him one evening after the children had gone to bed.

"How do you know?"

"Haven't you noticed? The kids have picked up the tune and are humming it all the time."

After that Eugene began to watch for their reaction. What Ferne said was true. If they liked a song well enough to hum or sing it at home, the chances were good that it would catch on. If they did not, the song probably would not become very popular. It was amazing to him that they were such a good gauge for judging his work.

When Diane was just old enough to want to help Ferne, she had a lot of trouble remembering where to place the silverware. No matter how many times her mother told her, she got it mixed up. To help her, Eugene wrote a little song:

"The fork goes on the left,
The spoon goes on the right.
The knife is placed beside the spoon
To make a pretty sight."

She giggled when he sang it to her. And after that Eugene could always tell when she was setting the table—he would hear her singing that merry little ditty.

116

It was a tremendous encouragement to the entire family to have Eugene working again. It was not so much that he again was able to provide for them, although Ferne had to admit that she was human enough to think about that. And the children were young enough to have complete trust in their father. Eugene had always taken care of them. Therefore, they supposed he always would. So, his being able to meet their physical needs was not a major concern. What encouraged them was that they all knew what his work meant to him and could see how happy he was at being able to arrange and compose once more. They constantly thanked God for that.

Having Eugene's bed in the dining room on the main floor worked out very well. At first the family ate their meals on a card table beside his bed. Later, when the children got bigger, they opted for television trays, but the result was the same. They were together as a family. Ferne would sit beside Eugene so that she could feed him at the same time the rest were eating. He was able to hear their meal-time conversations, listen to their devotions, and enter into everything.

They sat in his room at night, watching television or listening to the radio or the stereo. They played games in his room, and when company came they entertained there. It was not done solely for Eugene's benefit. They all enjoyed having him with them. They valued his advice and his contributions to their discussions. That he was bedridden and blind did not change his position in the family. He was still Ferne's husband, the children's father, and the head of their home.

Eugene knew when Bruce or Bryan had a tough test coming up and when Diane had a misunderstanding with a girl friend. He knew about the parties at church and at school. He knew when Bruce and Bryan were having problems, and he was

117

in charge of the discipline in the family. If the children did something they shouldn't, they had to face their father.

Even when they were quite small and might have been tempted to run away or defy him because he was immobile and could not catch or spank them, they quaked at having him raise his voice against them. And when they were disciplined—which was probably as often as most children their age were disciplined, because they were normal children—they suffered as though he had taken a whip to them.

The children have always gone to Eugene for advice, and for selfish reasons Ferne appreciated it. His judgment had always been so much better than hers, she thought. His way with them always seemed so firm and sure. Their attitude toward him and his discipline and counsel was no different from what it would have been if he were completely well.

The children were never ashamed of him and always brought their friends home. And Eugene and Ferne have always been pleased to have them bring their friends to the house. Some were uneasy at first about coming, embarrassed by Eugene's physical condition, but most of them acted as though they were in a home in which the father was healthy and well. Eugene enjoyed kidding with them, and it was gratifying to him to be accepted by the friends their children played with and to have some of those same friends stop by to ask his advice. "Isn't it great?" he asked Ferne the first time it happened. "That's one of the highest compliments he could have paid me."

It was not merely a lack of shame that made the children willing to bring their friends home. There was genuine pride in being the son or daughter of Eugene Clark. "Man," Bruce said one time. "You ought to see the look on the faces of people when they learn that I'm Eugene Clark's son." Ferne knew exactly what he meant. She had experienced the same pride in being Eugene's wife.

Ferne used to marvel at the way the children accepted their father's physical infirmities and the limitations they placed on the family activities. Then she realized that it was largely because of his attitude. He accepted without rancor or bitterness his blindness and his confinement to his bed. He laughed and joked with them, "watched" television with them, and kidded with their friends. Theirs was a normal home in every respect except Eugene's lack of sight and his immobility. Even when he had pain and discouragements, he did not burden the boys and Diane with them.

Ferne tried in other ways to keep her husband aware of things and what was going on around them, to help keep him interested in the world outside his room. She knew how much he had loved working in the yard and how interested he had been in growing things when he was able to take care of their yard and garden. With that in mind, she made a habit of describing the scene from their windows.

"Oh, Eugene," she would say, "you ought to see the yard this morning. The roses on both ends of the fence—the white ones—are in full bloom. The pink roses that were on the back of the arbor we used to have are also blooming, and the peonies are out. Those bushes are loaded with blossoms. And the Pauls Scarlet roses on the fence are just beginning to open up. I can see four little pears on our tree, and the grass is getting so tall that we're going to have to cut it again."

She did not limit her descriptions to the yard, either. If a little boy rode by on his tricycle, she described him and what he was doing, even to the puppy that tagged along behind. Eugene in turn

119

would ask about things in the yard, such as whether the lilacs were in bloom and whether the dandelions needed digging.

In the fall, Ferne would describe the leaves, the boys playing football in the street, and the first snow. She soon did not think of Eugene's blindness as an infirmity—only as a fact that they had to acknowledge.

Eugene cannot remember when he first got the idea for "Nothing Is Impossible." He had jotted down a few lines of lyrics and a bit of the tune and thrown them in the wire basket on the piano in his office. That was before his health deteriorated so rapidly in 1963. From time to time he would look at it and do a little work on the chorus, but it was not put all together. For some reason he was unable to finish it. Perhaps he was not ready to write about the theme. He had some troubled water to cross before he could fully realize that when one trusts in God, the statement is literally true: *Nothing Is Impossible!*

The idea lay in the basket, untouched and forgotten, until the time came to clean out his desk because it was apparent that he would be unable to return to the office. One of the secretaries sorted his personal items into one pile and the things that belonged to the Broadcast into another. She had almost finished the task when she found the basket he used for his ideas. She would read one and ask him if he wanted to keep it or throw it away. Then she would pick up the next. Toward the bottom of the pile she found "Nothing Is Impossible," the barest hint of an idea scrawled on a piece of foolscap.

"Do you want it, Gene?" she asked.

He thought momentarily. "Nothing is impossible," he repeated. "That sounds interesting. I may do something with it. I'd better keep it."

Hearing the sketchy notes he had made to record the idea months before started his mind working. As he lay in his bed he began to think about the theme, playing with words as he strove to develop lyrics that would speak his convictions on the subject. He wrote the chorus and verses and composed the music for them.

They used the song at the Broadcast, but there seemed to be no special interest in it afterward, so it lay around for a while. That may seem strange in view of what happened later, but its time had not yet come. That is occasionally the situation with songs. Some take off immediately and skyrocket to success so suddenly that everyone is amazed. Others will lie around for a while without impressing anybody, and then, after being all but forgotten, they will attract interest and increase in popularity.

"Nothing Is Impossible" fell into the latter group. After several years with little activity on it, Eugene received a letter one day from the secretary of the Moody Bible Institute's Alumni Association. The Institute was featuring alumni musicians at its Founders Week conference that year, and Eugene was being asked to write a song for the conference. He did not have any new ideas that interested him enough to go to work on them immediately, but he thought of "Nothing Is Impossible." He took another critical look at it, cleaned up the lyrics and harmony, and sent it in.

It was sung on Founder's Week Tuesday, which is Alumni Day. The hymn became immediately popular for some reason and became the theme song of the rest of the conference. It was sung at every meeting. There were so many personal comments and letters afterward, expressing gratitude for the blessing the song brought, that the alumni association printed forty thousand copies and sent one along with each letter that went out to the Institute's constituents. All of that got the Broadcast interested again, and they recorded it in one of their new stereo albums.

Cliff Barrow's secretary told him about the song, and he liked it so well that he played it for Billy Graham and the other members of their evangelistic team. They asked for permission to feature it in their Portland, Oregon, crusade and used it in Pittsburgh and several other campaigns as well. They also used it as a giveaway offer on a brief series of telecasts. They put it out as sheet music in a joint project with the Broadcast.

From the first, Eugene knew about the arrangement with the Billy Graham Association and that there would be some money coming to the Broadcast from it, but he never once thought that anything would come his way. After all, he had been on Broadcast time when he wrote the song and had been paid for working on it. He knew that it belonged to them. He was excited about having a song of his used so widely, however.

A few weeks after the deal with Graham was completed, Mr. Epp and Mr. Jones came out to the house to see Eugene. He suspected something unusual was happening when Ferne showed them into his room. They both had been to the house many times, but never together that he could remember, and certainly not during working hours. But here they were, sitting beside his bed, discussing the weather. Eugene and Ferne still did not know why the two men had come, but they were both aware of one fact: they were not there to talk about the possibility of rain that night. After a few minutes, Mr. Epp said he had something to tell them.

"It has always been Broadcast policy," he began, "and this is true of other businesses and organizations as well, that the work people produce during their regular hours belongs to the employer. That's the basis we have operated on in the past. Then this arrangement with the Billy Graham Association involving your song came up. We have been discussing it at length and have decided that we should share the royalty we have received for the use of 'Nothing Is Impossible.'"

"That's very kind of you," Eugene told him, "but you don't have to do that. You paid me to write the song. It belongs to you."

"We know we don't have to give it to you," Mr. Jones said, "but we want to." He took a check from his billfold and handed it to Ferne. "This is for half the amount we received from them."

She took it and glanced at it—almost casually, she told Eugene later. "Thank you," she said. Then she saw how large it was. "But there's an error somewhere. The decimal point is in the wrong place."

Mr. Epp smiled. "How large do you think it should be?" he asked.

She shrugged. "Probably fifty dollars."

She would have given the check back, but Mr. Jones stopped her with a gesture. "No," he said. "It's not in error."

"But—But—" she stammered. Her voice choked, and even though Eugene could not see her, he knew that tears were running down her cheeks. "But it's made out for five thousand dollars."

"That's right!"

How they thanked God! When Eugene first became blind and was confined to his bed, insurance took care of the house payments. There was a five year limit on that, however, and now that period was almost over. They were concerned about having to resume making those payments. They had been concerned, that is, until that afternoon. The five thousand dollars Mr. Epp and Mr. Jones brought to them was enough to take care of their most pressing bills and knock a big chunk out of the balance they owed on the house. Now they would have no difficulty paying it off.

But that is not the only way the directors of the Broadcast have helped the Clarks. They have allowed Eugene to work part-time which has kept his life and health insurance in force. And, when they decided to switch to another insurance company, they insisted, as a condition of getting the life insurance policies for the Broadcast employees, that Eugene be accepted as an employee. That also qualified him for major-medical insurance.

11

Those Happy Years

Before the Clark family began spending their summers at Maranatha Bible Camp near North Platte, Nebraska, they sensed that they needed a change from the routine of being in their own home month after month. So one day they borrowed a station wagon from a friend and moved, including Eugene and his hospital bed, over to his parents' home for a few weeks. They did that for several years, as soon as school was out. It was a change for all of them, and it brightened May with anticipation. That the Hugh Clarks lived only in another part of Lincoln did nothing to lessen the excitement. Ferne looked forward to it as much as the children did. It gave her an opportunity to be free of the responsibility of caring for Eugene for a few days so that she could spend time with the children alone, doing what they wanted to do.

She had always tried to spend time with the boys and Diane during the year, taking them places and doing things with them that Eugene would have done had he been able. During those two weeks, however, she made a special effort to spend even more time with them. There were frequent fishing trips to one of the little lakes in or near Lincoln.

"We never seemed to catch any fish, Mom," Bruce said, remembering those times when they were reminiscing not long ago, "but we sure had fun."

In spite of those visits to his parents' home, Eugene longed for Maranatha. The Bible camp had been such an important part of his life that he longed to get back there, even for a few days, during the camping season. But it did not seem possible. Both he and Ferne thought that Maranatha was one part of his life that was closed and locked against him. He tried to shut it out of his mind, but they found themselves talking about it with increasing frequency as the summer season approached.

And once again, God did the seemingly impossible for them. Whether He laid it on the heart of Pastor Olsen, who was by then director of the camp, to provide them a place to stay at camp so they could go there and enjoy it, or whether Pastor Olsen knew Eugene well enough to sense his deep longing to be part of Maranatha again, they do not know. But he made it possible for them to go to camp for several years, enjoying the facilities of the camp and eventually having a place they could use as their own.

At first they stayed in one of the three houses owned by the camp association. Pastor Olsen offered them the use of his own home, but Eugene would not accept. It would have caused Pastor Olsen great inconvenience to live with members of the staff in one of the other homes on the grounds. It was difficult enough, they realized, to allow them to use any of the homes when they were so needed.

Eugene and Ferne began to pray about housing at the camp. Not long after that, Pastor Olsen talked with Eugene's father about the possibility of building a place for them at Maranatha. When the cost estimate made it apparent that such a solution was not possible, Olsen asked Hugh Clark to ex-

126

plore the possibility of getting them a trailer home in Lincoln. The cost of getting a mobile home and installing air conditioning, a washer, dryer, and public address system was more than nine thousand dollars, but that proved to be the most economical solution. Everything was paid for by Eugene's and Ferne's friends who came to Maranatha. And, not surprisingly, the site chosen for the mobile home was exactly the spot that Diane and Ferne had decided was the most beautiful on the entire grounds and the place that they would select for a summer home if it were possible to have one. It was on a gentle, sloping hill, with the little lake at their front door. To their knowledge they had not mentioned their choice of a location for their home to anyone.

The children loved Maranatha as much as Eugene and Ferne, in spite of the difficulties that going to camp all summer created for them when they returned to Lincoln in the fall. Their friends had made new friends during the summer, and they had the problem of being accepted again. Eugene called it their culture shock. Still, they enjoyed being at Maranatha.

Bryan especially enjoyed the camp. He loved to fish, and the lake out front was like a magnet, constantly drawing his attention. It seemed to Ferne that their younger son smelled of fish from the time they got to camp in the spring until they packed to go home just before the fall school session began. His only regret in all his fishing was that his father could not enjoy it with him. But he even worked out a way for Eugene to enjoy his fun. With the help of his older brother he rigged up a second pole, complete with line, bobber, and hook. He baited each hook with the juiciest worms he could find and threw the lines into the water a few feet apart.

"Now, Mom," he said, "you've got to help me push Dad's bed in front of the window."

At first Ferne did not understand what he was about and asked him.

"Dad and I are goin' to be fishin'," he told her with a look that indicated he did not expect her to understand such things. "The pole by the tree belongs to Dad. The other one's mine." When they had Eugene's bed in a location that suited Bryan, he pulled up a chair and sat down. "I'll watch for you, Dad," he said, "and tell you when you get a bite."

A few moments later one of the bobbers began to wiggle and dance on the mirrored water.

"Dad!" Bryan whispered, his body tensing. "Dad! You're gettin' a bite!"

The bobber went under the water, and the boy dashed out the door and down the grassy slope to the water's edge. Triumphantly he came back with a wriggling bullhead that was seven or eight inches long.

"Look at him, Dad!" he exlaimed. "Just look at him! He's a real beaut!" No deep-sea fisherman was ever more proud of his catch. He insisted on helping Bruce clean Eugene's fish, and the two of them— Eugene and Bryan—had a taste of fish for supper.

That fishing time set the pace for Bryan's summer. He and his dad fished, day after day. That Eugene could not handle the pole or see it or his fish made no difference to his younger son. He and his dad were fishing . That was all that mattered.

Pastor Olsen gave Bruce his first job. He may have done it because Bruce was Eugene's son. Olsen knew the family was on the grounds all summer and that the children needed something to occupy their time. With nothing to do, they would get bored and might not want to come back. So, he hired the boy to work around the camp.

Although it was likely that Bruce got his job because of who he was, the favoritism shown to him ended there. He was put to work with the others, maintaining the camp. The work was difficult. They mowed endless stretches of lawn that had to be mowed again as soon as the job was done. They raked and pulled weeds and picked up trash. They pushed brooms and vacuumed and scrubbed. And when the camps were in session, they washed dishes and helped with the work in the kitchen.

It was not long before Pastor Olsen promoted Bruce to a position of leadership. "I know he's younger than those we usually promote to authority," the pastor-camp director explained to Eugene, "but he has the qualities we look for in filling that job." And he must have done well at it. He was able to hold the position and was also given added duties. Gradually his wages were raised until he was getting twice or three times the amount he started at. Yet Pastor Olsen always said that the children made a real financial sacrifice to work at camp.

Bruce, Bryan, and Diane did not look at it that way, however. They still talk about the good times they had during those summers at Maranatha and the spiritual depth it gave them. Ferne has always thought that they have been close to the Lord as they have grown older, in large part, because of the influence the camp had on them.

As Bryan matured he was big for his age and stronger than most of the children in his class at school, which got him jobs around camp that required strength; but nobody ever heard him complain about that. Diane was given a chance at the telephone switchboard and did so well, despite her youth, that they kept her on that job and others for several years.

It was not just the children who liked being at

Maranatha. Ferne was delighted to see the change that came over Eugene during the time they were there. Although they did not weigh him before and after his stay at Maranatha, it was apparent to her that he had gained weight.

The Clark children inherited their parents' musical ability and got into music at school as soon as they were old enough. Ferne has seldom missed one of their public appearances. Eugene has not missed many either: when Ferne goes to a musical event, a small tape recorder goes along. And when the event is over, the entire family gathers in his room to listen to the tape. They have not made a big point of doing that. Eugene cannot even recall asking the children to join them when he and Ferne listen to the tape. The children have done so because they wanted to be there.

"Just listen, Dad," one of them would say, chuckling. "Listen to the saxophone on this part. He really flubbed it! Here it is. Now, listen."

And they would all laugh at the saxophone player's mistake. They laughed not because they thought it was funny that someone else would make a blunder, but because they all had done similar things on numerous occasions and knew how he felt. Or perhaps there was a place where the music went very well, or where one of them had done a particularly outstanding bit of playing. They would call Eugene's attention to those places, too. When the number was finished, they would discuss the way it had been played and what could have been done to improve it.

As the years passed, both Eugene and Ferne grew quite concerned about the lack of space on the main floor of their home. Eugene in particular needed more space. Their dining room had been small, even for its original purpose, and now that they had Eugene's bed in it, it was woefully inadequate. There was no way they could provide him any privacy if anyone else was in the house, and there was scarcely room for all of them to gather around his bed.

They talked the space problem over at length one night after the children had gone to bed. They decided that the ideal solution would be to build another room onto the main floor, a room that would be large enough for them to put Eugene's bed in it and still have space for the rest of the family. They did not need or want anything fancy—just something that would provide extra space.

"Let's pray about being able to build on, Ferne," Eugene suggested. "Only, we shouldn't let anyone know about it. Pastor Lehman has already raised money to get us another car when the old one went kaput, and the people at the Broadcast and the church and at camp have done so much for us. We don't want them to do any more."

They began to pray secretly about their need. They did not even tell Bruce, Bryan, and Diane because they were afraid that word would leak out, and they did not want that. For two or three months they talked to God about it without any visible sign that He had heard their petitions. Then one morning, Pastor Olsen called Eugene from his home in North Platte.

"God woke me up in the middle of the night thinking about you," he said. "He made me aware that you have to have more space. With your permission I'm going to let some of your friends know that you need a larger house or a room built on the main floor."

Eugene could not even speak for a time; he was so moved by what was happening. When he did speak, he told Pastor Olsen about their prayers. "We've been very well satisfied with our present home," he said. "We like the neighborhood and the arrangement of the rooms. In fact, we like everything about it except that there isn't quite enough space on the main floor. Ferne and I have been thinking and praying about building on a simple room that would not be too expensive. It would only have to be large enough so we can all use it and still have my bed in it."

"We want exactly what God wants you to have," Pastor Olsen told him.

Pastor Olsen came down to Lincoln in a few days and conferred with their pastor, Curt Lehman, and Mr. Epp. They put out word that they were going to help the Clarks add a room to their house. What happened then amazed everyone. As soon as people heard about it they responded. Eugene and Ferne had been thinking in terms of four or five thousand dollars for the total cost of the addition, but God had other ideas. As the money poured in, Pastor Lehman went to a contractor in the church and talked with him about it.

"If you're going to do anything, Pastor," he said bluntly, "do it right. As for myself, I wouldn't want to have any part of it unless the addition could be built in such a way that it will not only give them the space they need but will also be an asset to the house. We want to increase its value, not leave it as it is or decrease it."

The contractor looked at the plans Ferne and Eugene had sketched and offered some suggestions to them. "First of all," he said, "the structure of the house is such that we are going to have to put in deep footings. You'll have to have the side walls anyway. If we dig out the space in the center we can make a nice-sized room for you in the basement, and about the only additional cost you'll have will be for the excavation and a cement floor."

He had other suggestions as work progressed. A bathroom was installed in the addition. The new addition was paneled and, at Pastor Olsen's insistence, a fireplace was put in. The furnace was not large enough to handle the extra load, so it was replaced and the house was air conditioned.

All the money that came in came from the Clarks' friends. And not only were all the bills paid for an addition that was far more functional than they had planned, but there was also enough left over to pay off the balance on the house loan. What a day of rejoicing there was in the Clark home when they were able to burn the mortgage in the fireplace!

12

Alumnus of the Year

Although Eugene had been able to hear the church services by special telephone line for several years, no one would have criticized him for not helping with the responsibilities that face the average member of a congregation. After all, he was unable to get out to the meetings. No one really expected him to carry a portion of the work load. But he has. He has served on the music committee, among others. The only concession to his affliction has been that the meetings he is supposed to attend are held in the Clark home.

"If anyone thinks Eugene is unaware of what's going on or that he is a 'rubber stamp' for the rest of the committee," Pastor Lehman says, "they don't know him very well. He makes up his own mind and is not backward about expressing his approval or opposition to matters under consideration. He is a real asset to any board he is on."

In addition to serving on the music committee for several years, he has done some arranging for the choir and special groups. And at Pastor Lehman's insistence, he has been writing a devotional column for the congregational newsletter for the past several years. "When he writes about suffering or trusting God," Pastor Lehman says, "people listen. No one else I know can hope to write with the same authority on the subject that he does." Although the mailing list has fewer than seven hundred fifty names and most of those who receive it live within the immediate area, the church hears from men and women all over the country who write to say what a blessing Eugene's short thoughts have been to them.

On a number of occasions Pastor Lehman has used Eugene for counseling. "Whenever I have individuals or a couple come to me, wallowing in self-pity and feeling that they have more troubles than anyone else in all the world, I see to it that they get to meet Eugene," he said. "If it is convenient, I will phone and make an appointment or ask if it's all right if we come. At other times I'll bring them over or even send them. I don't have to prepare him ahead of time. His own optimism is so steady that it isn't necessary to check first to see if he is depressed or discouraged, which could have the opposite effect to what we want to have on those we are trying to help."

Letters are constantly arriving at the Broadcast from those who have found help and encouragement from the way Eugene has faced his affliction. Some mention reading about him in the *Good News Broadcaster* or some other publication, but often he has not known how they learned about him. Not that it mattered. "What difference does it make?" he usually asks Ferne when she speculates about such things. "All that really counts is that they have found help and encouragement and been drawn closer to Jesus Christ."

Ferne will never forget the afternoon in the late fall of 1972 when Eugene got a phone call from Ken McQuere, director of the Moody Bible Institute Alumni Association. That in itself was not unusual.

136

He and Eugene were good friends, and he occasionally phoned to chat for a few minutes. This time, however, he had a strange request. "Gene," he said, "would you put Ferne on the phone, too?"

She was perplexed as she went into the other room to pick the extension phone. Usually no one wanted to talk to her. Eugene said later that the only thing he could figure was that they needed some music written. Once in a while they phoned him when they needed a special number. But that did not make sense, either. He handled all those matters himself. Never before had they asked her to get on the phone with him.

"I've got something I want to tell both of you," McQuere said. "The alumni committee has been meeting. They have selected Eugene as Alumnus of the Year."

The line went silent. There was no sound from either Eugene or Ferne. Finally Ken said to Ferne, "What do *you* think of this, Ferne?"

She was dumbfounded but was able to blurt, "All I can say is that you certainly chose the right man."

Eugene was aware that McQuere was waiting for him to reply, but he could not. Ferne said it was the first time since they started going together that she ever saw him speechless. He knew all about the Alumnus of the Year award. It is the big event of Founder's Week at Moody Bible Institute, and it climaxes the entire Alumni Day with its announcement in the evening meeting. Great care is taken to keep the choice secret. On other occasions the recipient was not even aware of having been chosen until the announcement was actually made.

Eugene could not imagine that he would even be considered for the award. He knew Ken McQuere and a few others around the Institute quite well, but he did not suppose that anyone outside his little circle of friends even knew that he existed. That made the announcement even more of a shock to him.

Eugene could understand why they had to reveal the committee's decision to them. He would not be able to go in to receive the award, as much as he would have liked to. Ferne would have to accept it for him. And there was no way they could have induced her to make the trip without spelling it out to them. That was the reason for the phone call.

"And remember," Ken repeated before hanging up, "we have to keep this secret from everyone. Don't even tell any other members of your family. We can't take a chance on this leaking out."

They knew it would not be easy to keep that promise, but they told the news to no one except Eugene's cousin, Dr. Robert Clark, who teaches in the Christian education department at the Institute. Ken had agreed to that. After all, Ferne and Bruce had to have someone to look after them when they arrived in Chicago.

Eugene was more shocked than Ferne at the honor that Moody Bible Institute was according him. She knew the kind of person he was and what he had accomplished in the field of music. Still, it took some getting used to. As she lay on the couch in the living room, unable to sleep for the excitement coursing through her veins, it scarcely seemed possible that it was happening. She was afraid that she would wake up to find that it was all a tantalizingly beautiful dream that would disappear when the first rays of morning sunlight shone through the window.

However, that was not the case. It was real. McQuere wanted Ferne to bring Bruce along. He would be a companion on the trip, and, because he was in high school, he would furnish an excellent cover for the real purpose of the visit. Anyone seeing them there would quite naturally assume that they had come to take part in Founder's Week and to let Bruce look over the school at the same time.

Again the alumni director stressed the importance of secrecy. He did not want to meet them at the airport, and they were not supposed to approach or talk to him before the evening meeting at which the announcement was to be made. If anyone saw them having any sort of contact with him, word could leak out, and they wanted Eugene's selection to be a surprise to everyone.

The day Ferne and Bruce arrived in Chicago, Dr. Clark's son met them at the airport and took them into the city to a motel a block from the Institute. The next morning Ferne and Bruce walked up to the Institute, where Dr. Clark met them in the lobby. Both Bruce and Ferne were so excited that they could scarcely stand it, and they were afraid that they might do or say something that would give away the true purpose of their visit.

Dr. Clark spent the entire day with them and nobody thought anything about it, especially when people learned that he and Eugene were cousins. He took them through the school, showing them the library, the classrooms, and the lounges. Ferne was particularly interested in the studios of WMBI, because Eugene had spent so much time in them when he was going to school there.

That trip was not Ferne's first visit to the Institute. She had been there once before, shortly after she and Eugene were married. They had only been through a portion of it then, however, and there had been so many changes since that it would not have made any difference if she had seen it all before. Every department had been upgraded and expanded since her first visit.

At the noon alumni banquet she met John Peterson and his wife, Marie. John and Eugene had been good friends for years, and she was thrilled at the opportunity to meet him. She also got to meet Mr.

Broman, who had been dean of men when Eugene was at the Institute as a student, and Dr. George Schuler. Dr. Clark took her over to his table. "Dr. Schuler," he said, "I want you to meet Eugene Clark's wife."

His eyes fixed on her for an instant, and then his entire being seemed to light up. *"You're who?"* he boomed in his great, loud voice.

She cringed self-consciously, as she could imagine that everyone in the place was staring at her. The thought came to her that if everyone spoke as loudly as Dr. Schuler, public address systems never would have become popular.

"I'm Eugene Clark's wife," she said.

With that he grabbed her hand and pumped it excitedly. "Eugene never did have much to do with the girls around here."

She did not know whether he thought she needed that assurance or not.

"I will never forget Eugene Clark!" he continued. Then he turned to Bruce and went through the same routine. "So you're Eugene's son! I knew your dad well. A good student and a great musician!"

Bruce could not have agreed more heartily with that assessment of his dad, but he confessed afterward that he was so embarrassed that he felt like crawling under the table.

Somehow the day passed, and then they went to Torrey-Gray Auditorium for the evening meeting, during which the award was to be made. The alumni department arranged for Bruce and Ferne to be seated near the front where they would be close to the platform without being conspicuous. Ferne was thankful for the telephone hookup that they had so thoughtfully provided for Eugene. It was a thrill for Bruce and her to be there and see what was going on, but actually the evening was Eugene's. They were pleased that Eugene, Bryan, and Diane did not have to miss it, even though they had been unable to make the trip to Chicago.

Eugene heard them say some things about his life and his accomplishments for the Lord. Bruce and Ferne got more excited with each passing moment, especially as people began to whisper to each other, "I think it's Eugene Clark." "It has to be Eugene Clark they're talking about." His wife and son squirmed and twisted, so proud that they felt as if they were about to explode. Ferne was sure that anyone looking at them could have seen the truth in their faces. They had been able to refrain from speaking, but they could not keep the excitement from their eyes.

Then Eugene was announced as the winner of the year's award, and Ferne was called to the platform to receive a wooden plaque on which was mounted a beautifully handwritten parchment. Going up on that platform in her husband's place was one of the greatest thrills of Ferne's life. She was sure it was the same for Bruce, who had been called up with her.

Mrs. McQuere came and pinned a beautiful corsage on Ferne, and then Ferne was asked to say a few words. Bob Clark said afterward that he kept wondering how she could keep so composed. She had shed a few tears, but she remained calm. "My calmness had to come from the Lord," she told him. "It's not normal for me to be calm in a situation like that."

"I might have been calm on the outside," Bruce said, "but I was shaking, too. My knees were knocking so much that I was afraid people would see that my pants were shaking."

The next day they had a grand tour of the entire school, and it was exciting. When they were introduced to strangers before the award, the people would acknowledge the introduction politely and that would be that. But after Eugene had been presented the Alumnus of the Year award, Ferne was introduced as Eugene Clark's wife. Suddenly she was someone very special, a person others wanted to meet.

That popularity made her recall a visit that she and the children had made to a small church in Lincoln a number of years before when they were small. After the service her friends flocked around to visit with her. When they got into the car to go home, Bruce said, "Boy, Mom, you sure must be popular. Everybody came up and talked to you."

With that one of the other two said, "Oh, didn't you know? Daddy made Mommy famous." That was the way she felt as they whisked her around the Institute.

That afternoon someone showed her a copy of the *Moody Student,* the student publication that comes out once a week. They had a picture of Eugene and a long, complimentary story about him on the front page.

"I just have to have some of these," she told Dr. Clark.

"Well," he said, "let's go up to the office and see if they have any extras."

He introduced her at the office and said that she would like to take home a few *Moody Student*s.

"I think that can be arranged," the woman at the desk said. "How many do you want?"

"As many as you can spare."

A strange look crossed her face. "Did you just want them for the weekend?" she asked.

At that moment Ferne realized the other woman thought she was talking about real, live students. She supposed the receptionist in the office thought she wanted to introduce them to Eugene or something. She got her *Moody Students*, all right, but the kind that she could roll up and carry under her arm.

13

"The Greatest of These"

Eugene had been interested in foreign missions since he was a child growing up in the missions-minded Berean Fundamental Church in North Platte, Nebraska. His concern and interest were fanned by his years at Moody Bible Institute and Wheaton College, and they burst into flame at the Broadcast, where missions and missionaries have always played an important role. One of the greatest disappointments of his life was that he had been unable, because of his health, to become a missionary.

Then one day a visitor asked him and Ferne about the various translations of his music into other languages. They began to name them. "All three cantatas were translated into Chinese," Ferne said, "and one is in Polish, one is in Portuguese, and one is in Spanish."

"And some of my hymns and other songs are in Japanese, Greek, Dutch, Italian, and a number of African languages," Eugene added. "I—I would guess they're in at least twenty different languages and dialects—perhaps more." Even as he spoke he became aware of something he had never fully understood before. He could scarcely wait until they were alone to tell Ferne about it. "All these years," he said, his voice trembling with emotion, "I've been disturbed by the fact that I have been unable to serve God as a missionary. Now I see that, even though I have been unable to go in person, God has made it possible for me to go to many countries as a missionary through my music."

Her eyes grew misty. "And I've been privileged to tag along," she said.

Through her dad's constant concern for others, Diane developed an interest in those who had special problems. Ferne and Eugene were pleased when she came home and told them that she had decided to go to a class in "signing"* that was being held after school.

When Diane had been in the class for some time and had become quite proficient, the teacher called Eugene and Ferne and said that the university was making a film to use in teaching deaf children; she asked if Diane could try out for one of the parts. Diane was very excited—so much so that her parents were concerned about how she would take it if she lost out. Ferne went to her room and talked with her about it.

"You realize that a lot of kids are going to try out," Ferne told her, "and only a few will be able to appear in the film. So don't be disappointed if you don't get it." Then they prayed about it. When they finished praying, Ferne said, "Now, we have spent time asking the Lord to help you get the part. We must spend time thanking Him for His answer, whatever it happens to be."

"Oh, I have, Mom," Diane said quickly. "I have thanked Him and thanked Him and thanked Him."

*Signing is the skill of speaking through sign language, developed for use in communicating with those who have impaired hearing.

When the call finally came, Diane had won the leading role, and she turned in a very acceptable performance.

What Eugene and Ferne thought was even more important, however, was that Diane had learned a valuable lesson through the incident. She had learned that the Lord wants our hearts to be overflowing with thankfulness always, in the hard times as well as in the times when all is going well. Most people have to learn that lesson through adversity. Diane had the opportunity to learn it by thanking God for His answers before she knew how the tryouts were going to end.

Eugene has taught his family much in that area. Ferne says that had it not been for his example, she might very well have grown bitter and vindictive because of his health problems and the difficulties they all had because of them.

Because of Eugene's physical condition and the pain that is constantly with him, it is impossible for him to lay out plans for the future as most musicians do. He is not able to outline cantatas or new hymns that he hopes to write. Those things may come, but if they do it will have to be on a day-to-day basis as God gives him strength and moves him to work. However, the witness for Christ that has been so important throughout Eugene's adult life is still carried on. Only now it is Ferne who is doing it.

She had never thought that she would be able to do any public speaking. It was not the sort of thing she felt comfortable with, but she was asked to give a little talk to the women's fellowship in their church, and she did not think she could refuse. If it had been anything more than that, she said later, she would have turned down the request, but most of the women who would be there were friends. And the people in the church had been so close to them

147

over the years that she could not turn them down. So she went to the meeting, described some of the things that had happened to Eugene and her, and told how the Lord had used those things to reveal His love to them and bring them closer to Himself. She thought that one talk would be the end of it and was relieved when it was over, but someone who heard her invited her to speak to a group of mothers. Ferne tried to protest that she was not a public speaker, but they told her they wanted her to bring the same message that she had brought to the women's fellowship.

Some time later, Ferne was asked to speak to the Christian Women's Club in Lincoln. After that appearance the invitations increased steadily, coming from points throughout Nebraska, Iowa, and Kansas. Each speaking engagement was traumatic for her. She had to dredge up some of the more painful experiences from memory, and often, after she had spoken, she would have a great deal of difficulty getting to sleep at night. Then there was the problem of neglecting Eugene and the children and her home.

"I don't know what to do about accepting all these speaking engagements," she said to Eugene. "They're taking me away from home so much that it's beginning to bother me." Regardless of the other demands on her time, she felt that she could not neglect him or the children.

Eugene did not like to have her away, either. He had already told her how the hours dragged when she was away from home. "But we can't think about ourselves first, Ferne," he said. "We've got to consider what the Lord wants you to do. If He is in these speaking invitations that are coming to you, you dare not turn them down."

For a week or two they prayed earnestly about the matter, seeking God's guidance. The answer came

148

slowly, a gradual realization that God was prompting the Christian women's clubs in their area to ask her to speak. They were able to work out the problems caused by her being away from time to time, and she went out to speak wherever she was invited.

She soon learned that there was trouble everywhere that was far worse than that which her family faced. Eugene was bedfast and blind and, barring a miracle, would never improve. Yet they stood together as a Christian couple and family. They loved each other and faced the problems of life secure in the knowledge that they had each other. She could not have believed all the heartache of others had women not felt free to discuss their burdens with her. She never would have imagined there were so many women who were unenthusiastic about their marriages, who counted their wedding days as the time when their lives took a miserable turn and started to grow steadily worse. She had never known that so many men were unfaithful or that so many had torn their families apart with their drinking or gambling.

Women seemed to find strength hearing that God had seen Eugene and Ferne through some very difficult times. Hearing of the Clarks' experiences often gave them the encouragement they needed to carry on, serene in the trust that God would care for them and give them strength. One middle-aged wife and mother revealed to Ferne that her husband had made a habit of having one new lover after another. There was nothing she could do to induce him to be true to her, and she did not know how to handle the humiliation and sense of failure that engulfed her. "Now that I've heard you, Mrs. Clark," she said, "I know that God has the power to meet my needs and that He is concerned about what happens to me and will give me the strength to bear anything that

149

happens. I can go home and strive to be the best wife possible and keep my family together."

Another woman came to Ferne after one of the meetings and confided her problem. She was younger than Ferne by a dozen years and had three small children. "I've just learned that I have a very virulent form of cancer and have six months, at most, to live. Until tonight I haven't known how to cope with it. You'll never know what this evening has meant to me. Now I can go home and trust Christ to take care of my problems."

After Ferne spoke in Eugene's hometown of North Platte, five ladies indicated that they had made decisions for Christ. On the same trip she spoke in two more communities, and there were nine additional women who placed their trust in Christ. And so it went. God was making it abundantly clear that He wanted Ferne to tell their story to others.

There are some advantages to being blind that are not apparent to the sighted. Bruce was eight years old when Eugene last saw him. Eugene will always remember him as he was the day the lights went out and his vision blurred and dimmed. He will always remember Ferne as being young and beautiful. He will not have to see the wrinkles that age and the cares of this world will crease in her face. To him her hair will always be a beautiful red, devoid of gray.

And his parents: to him, his mother will always be beautiful and young. He is spared the hurt of seeing her youth fade and her body begin to hunch with infirmities and pain. His dad will always be vigorous and active, as he was at the time Eugene lost his sight.

And God has sharpened his senses, too. His hearing is keen and he has learned to make all sorts of deductions from the sounds around him. He can recognize Ferne's footsteps the instant he hears her, and he is able to know something about her mood by the way she walks. That quick tapping as she bustles about the house indicates she is vivacious and happy. When she is troubled, her footsteps are slower and measured. If she is disturbed or angry, her feet become hammers beating a fierce tattoo on the stairs and floor.

He knows the footsteps of strangers and those of each of their children, his parents, and Ferne's mother when she is with them. He can find joy in the cheery crackling of fire in the fireplace and in the chirping of the birds on early spring mornings.

His life is rich and full with the love of God, the love of a beautiful wife and three joyful Christian children, and the love of parents who love the Lord. He has the love and fellowship of an inner circle of friends and of those not quite so close but nonetheless very precious to him. His is truly a story of love.

At the Moody Bible Institute's 1978 Founder's Week conference, the theme was prophecy. Eugene wrote a new song for the occasion that became the theme song, "Alleluia He Will Come."

When Christ returns, if that should happen before God calls Eugene home, Eugene will have a new body and new eyes with which to look into the face of his Savior. Whether he is freed by death or by Christ's return does not really matter. He will be able to see and walk and run and play his beloved piano again. Until that happens, he will wait with a patience that is from God. "Even so, come, Lord Jesus" (Revelation 22:20b).

Moody Press, a ministry of the Moody Bible Institute, is designed for education, evangelization, and edification. If we may assist you in knowing more about Christ and the Christian life, please write us without obligation: Moody Press, c/o MLM, Chicago, Illinois 60610.

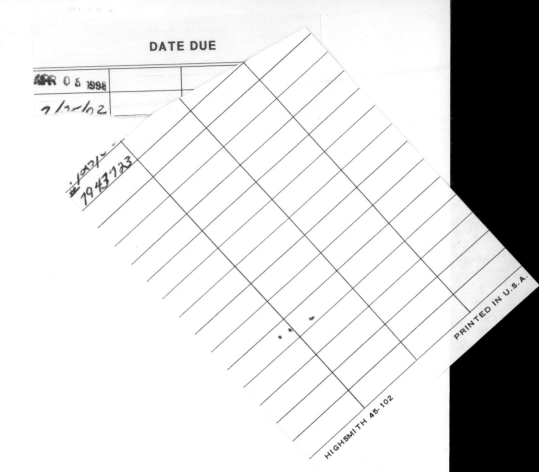